CO

CLASS NOTES
2

APPETIZERS & SOUPS
6

PASTA DISHES
20

ITALIAN ENTRÉES
44

SALADS & SIDE DISHES
62

DESSERTS
76

INDEX
94

Classic Meatball Soup (*page 16*)

Spinach Lasagna (*page 33*)

Tomato, Mozzarella & Basil Salad (*page 62*)

CLASS NOTES

In the last decade, Italian cuisine has gone from the usual spaghetti and meatballs to a favorite in America's kitchens with diverse dishes like tortellini in cream sauce and seafood marinara. In fact, Americans eat more than 4 billion pounds of pasta each year. That comes to more than 17 pounds per person. With pasta popularity at an all time high, more than 150 different shapes are available!

But Italian food is clearly more than just pasta. A true Italian meal is very different from the single, large plate of pasta many of us associate with Italian cooking. In Italy, there is no main course as we know it, but rather a series of courses. *Antipasto*, which literally translated means "before the pasta," is the appetizer course and can be served either hot or cold. Soup may sometimes follow or replace the antipasto. The next course—*I Primi* or first course—usually consists of a pasta dish. *I Secondi* is the second course and features meat, poultry or fish. The pasta and meat courses are sometimes combined. The salad course or *Insalata* is served after the main portion of the meal to perk up tired tastebuds. *I Dolci*, which translates to "the sweets," is the dessert course usually served with an espresso or cappuccino.

The recipes in this publication include many traditional dishes of Italy and illustrate the variety of this delicious cuisine. Using authentic ingredients and cooking techniques, *Cooking Class Italian* shows even the novice cook how to achieve great results with easy step-by-step instructions and helpful how-to photographs.

COOKING PASTA

Dry Pasta: For every pound of dry pasta, bring 4 to 6 quarts of water to a full, rolling boil. Add 2 teaspoons salt, if desired. Gradually add pasta, allowing water to return to a boil. The boiling water helps circulate the pasta so that it cooks evenly. Stir frequently to prevent the pasta from sticking. Begin testing for doneness after 5 minutes of cooking. Pasta that is "al dente"—meaning "to the tooth"—is tender, yet firm. Draining the pasta as soon as it is done stops the cooking action and helps prevent overcooking. For best results, toss the pasta with sauce immediately after you drain it and serve within minutes. If the sauce is not ready, toss the pasta with some butter or oil to prevent it from becoming sticky.

Pasta in its dry, uncooked form can be stored almost indefinitely in a cool dry place.

Fresh Pasta: Homemade pasta takes less time to cook than dry pasta. Cook fresh pasta in the same manner as dry, except begin testing for doneness after 2 minutes. Many of the recipes in *Cooking Class Italian* show you how to make homemade pasta. Making pasta is fun and easy, but when time is short, dry pasta is a good substitute. What's important is that the pasta is never overcooked. Fresh pasta will last several weeks in the refrigerator or can be frozen for up to 1 month.

EQUIPMENT

Pastry Board: A slab made of marble or granite that is well suited for rolling dough and pastry because it is smooth and stays cool. A well-floured countertop or acrylic cutting board can also be used.

Pasta Machine: Pasta machines with hand-turned rollers are very useful in kneading and rolling pasta dough. Cutting attachments (fettuccine and angel hair are usually included) help to cut pasta evenly. Electric machines also mix the dough, however the pasta usually lacks the resilience of hand-worked dough and the machines are more expensive. Methods of making pasta by hand are also included in this publication.

Pastry Wheel: A straight or scalloped wheel with a handle that speeds the cutting of pastry or pasta shapes, such as ravioli. A sharp utility knife or pizza cutter can be substituted.

ITALIAN INGREDIENTS

These ingredients are normally available in Italian groceries. Many can be found in supermarkets and gourmet food stores.

Arborio Rice: Italian-grown short-grain rice that has large, plump grains with a delicious nutty taste. It is traditionally used for risotto dishes because its high starch content produces a creamy texture and it can absorb more liquid than regular- or long-grain rice.

Cannellini Beans: Large, white Italian kidney beans available both in dry and canned forms. Dried beans need to be soaked in water several hours or overnight to rehydrate before cooking; canned beans should be rinsed and drained to freshen the beans. Cannellini beans are often used in Italian soups, such as Minestrone. Great Northern beans make a good substitute.

Capers: Flower buds of a bush native to the Mediterranean. After the buds are sun-dried, they are pickled in a vinegar brine. Capers should be rinsed and drained before using to remove excess salt.

Eggplant: A cousin of the tomato, the eggplant is actually a fruit, though commonly thought of as a vegetable. Eggplants come in various shapes and sizes and their color can vary from deep purple to creamy ivory. However, these varieties are similar in taste and should be salted to remove their bitter flavor (technique on page 68). Choose firm, unblemished eggplants with a smooth, glossy skin. They should feel heavy for their size. Store in a cool, dry place and use within a day or two of purchase. Do not cut in advance since the flesh discolors rapidly.

Fennel: An anise-flavored, bulb-shaped vegetable with celerylike stems and feathery leaves. Both the base and stems can be eaten raw in salads or sautéed, and the seeds and leaves can be used for seasoning food. Purchase clean, crisp bulbs with no sign of browning and greenery should be a fresh green color. Store in the refrigerator, tightly wrapped in a plastic bag, for up to 5 days.

Hazelnuts (also called Filberts): Wild nuts that grow in clusters on the hazel tree. Italy is the leading producer of hazelnuts. For best results, remove the bitter brown skin that covers the nuts (technique on page 82). Store in an airtight container in a cool, dry place for up to 1 month or freeze for up to 1 year.

Italian Plum Tomatoes: A flavorful egg-shaped tomato that comes in red and yellow varieties. As with other tomatoes, they are very perishable. Choose firm tomatoes that are fragrant and free of blemishes. Ripe tomatoes should be stored at room temperature and used within a few days. Canned tomatoes are a good substitute when fresh ones are out of season.

Mascarpone Cheese: This buttery-rich double- to triple-cream cheese made with cow's milk is the creamiest of the Italian cheeses. When purchasing cheese, check the expiration date; store covered in the refrigerator.

Olive Oil: Extracted oil from tree-ripened olives used for both salads and cooking. Olive oils are graded by the level of acidity they contain. The best are cold-pressed and produce a low level of acidity. The highest grade is extra virgin olive oil, which contains a maximum of 1 percent acidity. Virgin olive oil contains up to a 3½ percent acidity level, and pure olive oil is a blend of virgin olive oil and refined residue. Olive oil does not improve with age; exposure to air and heat turns oil rancid. Store olive oil in a cool, dark place for up to 6 months or refrigerate for up to 1 year. Olive oil becomes cloudy when chilled; bring chilled olive oil to room temperature before using.

Pancetta: Italian bacon that is cured with salt and spices, but not smoked. It is slightly salty, comes in a sausagelike roll and is used to flavor sauces, pasta dishes and meats. Pancetta can be tightly wrapped and refrigerated for up to 3 weeks or frozen for up to 6 months.

Parmesan Cheese: A hard, dry cheese made from skimmed cow's milk. This cheese has a straw-colored interior with a rich, sharp flavor. The imported Italian Parmigiano-Reggiano has been aged at least 2 years, whereas domestic renditions are only aged 14 months. Parmesan cheese is primarily used for grating. While pre-grated cheese is available, it does not compare with freshly grated. Store Parmesan cheese pieces loosely in plastic and refrigerate for up to 1 week. Refrigerate freshly grated Parmesan cheese in an airtight container for up to 1 week.

Pine Nuts (also called Pignolias): These nuts are actually inside pine cones and Italian pine nuts come from the stone pine tree. Pine nuts have a light, delicate flavor and are a well known ingredient in the classic Italian pesto sauce. Store in an airtight container in the refrigerator for up to 3 months or freeze for up to 9 months.

Prosciutto: The Italian word for "ham," prosciutto is seasoned, salt-cured and air-dried (not smoked). Although the imported Parma can now be purchased in America, the less expensive domestic prosciutto is a good substitute. It is usually sold in very thin slices and eaten as a first course with melon slices and figs. It also can be added at the last minute to cooked foods, such as pasta and vegetables. Wrap tightly and refrigerate slices for up to 3 days or freeze for up to 1 month.

Radicchio: Mainly used as a salad green, this red-leafed Italian chicory has burgundy red leaves with white ribs. It grows in a small, loose head and has tender, but firm leaves. Radicchio has a slightly bitter flavor. Choose crisp heads with no sign of browning and store in a plastic bag in the refrigerator for up to 1 week. Radicchio may also be grilled, sautéed or baked.

Ricotta Cheese: A white, moist cheese with a slightly sweet flavor. It is rich, fresh and slightly grainy, but smoother than cottage cheese. Ricotta, which translated means "recooked," is made from heating the whey from another cooked cheese, such as mozzarella or provolone. Ricotta cheese is often used in lasagna and manicotti. Cottage cheese makes a good substitute, but with creamier results. When purchasing cheese, check the expiration date; store tightly covered in the refrigerator.

Venetian Canapés

12 slices firm white bread
5 tablespoons butter or margerine, divided
2 tablespoons all-purpose flour
½ cup milk
3 ounces fresh mushrooms (about 9 medium), finely chopped
6 tablespoons grated Parmesan cheese, divided
2 teaspoons anchovy paste
¼ teaspoon salt
⅛ teaspoon black pepper
Green and ripe olive slices, red and green bell pepper strips and rolled anchovy fillets for garnish

1. Preheat oven to 350°F. Cut circles out of bread slices with 2-inch round cutter. Melt 3 tablespoons butter in small saucepan. Brush both sides of bread circles lightly with butter. Bake bread circles on ungreased baking sheet 5 to 6 minutes per side until golden. Remove to wire rack. Cool completely. *Increase oven temperature to 425°F.*

2. Melt remaining 2 tablespoons butter in same small saucepan. Stir in flour; cook and stir over medium heat until bubbly. Whisk in milk; cook and stir 1 minute or until sauce thickens and bubbles. (Sauce will be very thick.) Place mushrooms in large bowl; stir in sauce, 3 tablespoons cheese, anchovy paste, salt and black pepper until well blended.

3. Spread heaping teaspoonful mushroom mixture on top of each toast round; place on ungreased baking sheets. Sprinkle remaining 3 tablespoons cheese over canapés, dividing evenly. Garnish, if desired.

4. Bake 5 to 7 minutes until tops are light brown. Serve warm.

Makes 8 to 10 servings (about 2 dozen)

Mediterranean Frittata

¼ cup olive oil
5 small yellow onions, thinly sliced
1 can (14½ ounces) whole peeled tomatoes, drained and chopped
¼ pound prosciutto or cooked ham, chopped
¼ cup grated Parmesan cheese
2 tablespoons chopped fresh parsley
½ teaspoon dried marjoram leaves, crushed
¼ teaspoon dried basil leaves, crushed
¼ teaspoon salt
Generous dash freshly ground black pepper
6 eggs
2 tablespoons butter or margarine
Italian parsley leaves for garnish

1. Heat oil in medium skillet over medium-high heat. Cook and stir onions in hot oil 6 to 8 minutes until soft and golden. Add tomatoes. Cook and stir over medium heat 5 minutes. Remove tomatoes and onions to large bowl with slotted spoon; discard drippings. Cool tomato-onion mixture to room temperature.

2. Stir prosciutto, cheese, parsley, marjoram, basil, salt and pepper into cooled tomato-onion mixture. Whisk eggs in small bowl; stir into prosciutto mixture.

3. Preheat broiler. Heat butter in large *broilerproof* skillet over medium heat until melted and bubbly; reduce heat to low.

4. Add egg mixture to skillet, spreading evenly. Cook over low heat 8 to 10 minutes until all but top ¼ inch of egg mixture is set; shake pan gently to test. *Do not stir.*

5. Broil egg mixture about 4 inches from heat 1 to 2 minutes until top of egg mixture is set. (Do not brown or frittata will be dry.) Frittata can be served hot, at room temperature or cold. To serve, cut into wedges. Garnish, if desired.

Makes 6 to 8 appetizer servings

Antipasto with Marinated Mushrooms

- **1 recipe Marinated Mushrooms (recipe follows)**
- **4 teaspoons red wine vinegar**
- **½ teaspoon dried basil leaves, crushed**
- **½ teaspoon dried oregano leaves, crushed**
- **Generous dash freshly ground black pepper**
- **¼ cup olive oil**
- **4 ounces mozzarella cheese, cut into ½-inch cubes**
- **4 ounces prosciutto or cooked ham, thinly sliced**
- **4 ounces Provolone cheese, cut into 2-inch sticks**
- **1 jar (10 ounces) pepperoncini peppers, drained**
- **8 ounces hard salami, thinly sliced**
- **2 jars (6 ounces each) marinated artichoke hearts, drained**
- **1 can (6 ounces) pitted ripe olives, drained**
- **Lettuce leaves (optional)**
- **Fresh basil leaves and chives for garnish**

1. Prepare Marinated Mushrooms; set aside.

2. Combine vinegar, basil, oregano and black pepper in small bowl. Add oil in slow steady stream, whisking until oil is thoroughly blended. Add mozzarella cubes; stir to coat. Marinate, covered, in refrigerator at least 2 hours. Wrap ½ of prosciutto slices around Provolone sticks; roll up remaining slices separately.

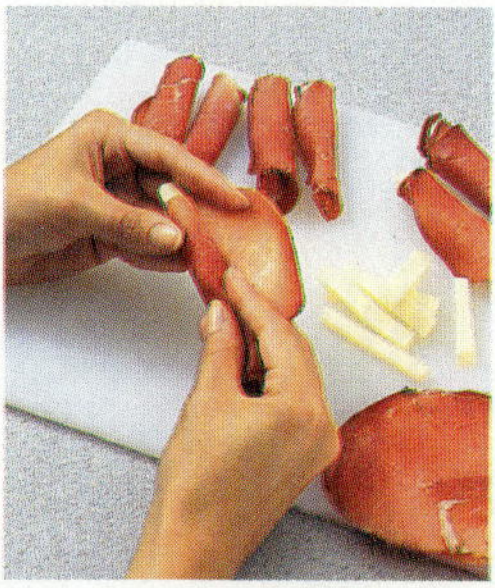

3. Drain mozzarella cubes; reserve marinade. Arrange mozzarella cubes, prosciutto-wrapped Provolone sticks, prosciutto rolls, marinated mushrooms, pepperoncini, salami, artichoke hearts and olives on large platter lined with lettuce, if desired. Drizzle reserved marinade over pepperoncini, artichoke hearts and olives. Garnish, if desired. Serve with small forks or wooden toothpicks.

Makes 6 to 8 servings

Marinated Mushrooms

- **3 tablespoons lemon juice**
- **2 tablespoons chopped fresh parsley**
- **½ teaspoon salt**
- **¼ teaspoon dried tarragon leaves, crushed**
- **Generous dash freshly ground black pepper**
- **½ cup olive oil**
- **1 clove garlic**
- **½ pound fresh medium mushrooms**

continued on page 12

Antipasto with Marinated Mushrooms, continued

1. To make marinade, combine lemon juice, parsley, salt, tarragon and pepper in medium bowl. Add oil in slow steady stream, whisking until oil is thoroughly blended.

2. Lightly crush garlic with flat side of chef's knife or mallet. Spear garlic with small wooden toothpick and add to marinade.

3. Slice stems from mushrooms; reserve stems for another use. Wipe mushroom caps clean with damp kitchen towel. Add mushrooms to marinade; mix well. Marinate, covered, in refrigerator 4 hours or overnight, stirring occasionally.

4. To serve, remove and discard garlic. Serve mushrooms on antipasto tray or as relish. Or, add mushrooms to tossed green salad, using marinade as dressing.

Makes about 2 cups

Cioppino

6 to 8 hard-shell clams
1 quart *plus* 2 tablespoons water, divided
1 cup dry white wine
2 onions, thinly sliced
1 rib celery, chopped
3 sprigs parsley
1 bay leaf
¾ pound ocean perch or snapper fillets
1 can (14½ ounces) whole peeled tomatoes, undrained
1 tablespoon tomato paste
1 clove garlic, minced
1 teaspoon dried oregano leaves, crushed
1 teaspoon salt
½ teaspoon sugar
⅛ teaspoon pepper
2 large ripe tomatoes
2 large potatoes
1 pound fresh halibut or haddock fillets
½ pound fresh medium shrimp
2 tablespoons chopped fresh parsley
Celery leaves for garnish

1. Scrub clams with stiff brush under cold running water. Soak clams in large bowl of cold water 30 minutes. Remove clams with slotted spoon; discard water. Repeat soaking 2 more times.

2. To make fish stock, combine 1 quart water, wine, onions, celery, parsley sprigs and bay leaf in 6-quart stockpot or Dutch oven. Bring to a boil over high heat; reduce heat to low. Add perch; uncover and gently simmer 20 minutes.

3. Strain fish stock through sieve into large bowl. Remove perch to plate with slotted spatula; set aside. Discard onions, celery, parsley sprigs and bay leaf.

4. Return stock to stockpot; press canned tomatoes and juice through sieve into stockpot. Discard seeds. Stir in tomato paste, garlic, oregano, salt, sugar and pepper. Simmer, uncovered, over medium-low heat 20 minutes.

continued on page 14

Cioppino, continued

5. Combine clams and remaining 2 tablespoons water in stockpot or large saucepan. Cover and cook over medium heat 5 to 10 minutes until clams open; remove clams immediately with metal tongs as they open. Discard any clams with unopened shells. Rinse clams; set aside.

6. Cut fresh tomatoes in half. Remove stems and seeds; discard. Coarsely chop tomatoes.

7. Peel potatoes; cut into ¾-inch cubes. Skin halibut; cut into 1½ × 1-inch pieces. Add fresh tomatoes, potatoes and halibut to soup mixture in stockpot. Bring to a boil over high heat; reduce heat to medium-low. Cover and cook 12 to 15 minutes until potatoes are fork tender.

8. Remove shells from shrimp under cold running water. To devein, cut shallow slit down back of shrimp; pull out and discard vein. Add shrimp to soup mixture in stockpot.

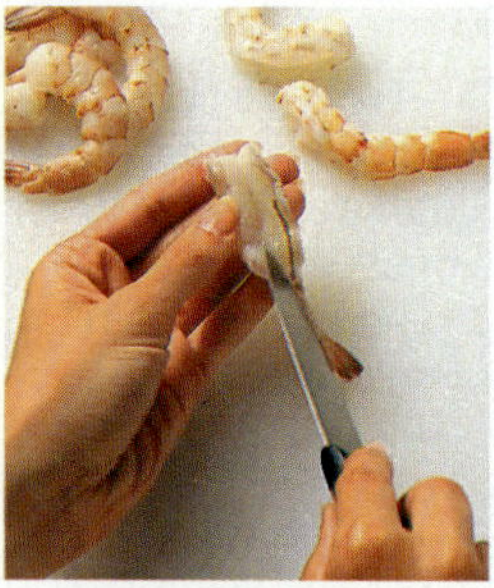

9. Cook over medium heat 1 to 2 minutes just until shrimp turn opaque and are cooked through. Flake reserved perch with fork; stir perch, reserved clams and chopped parsley into soup.

Garnish, if desired. Serve immediately.

Makes 6 to 8 servings (about 10 cups)

Classic Meatball Soup

- **2 pounds beef bones**
- **3 ribs celery**
- **2 carrots**
- **1 medium onion, cut in half**
- **1 bay leaf**
- **6 cups cold water**
- **1 egg**
- **4 tablespoons chopped fresh parsley, divided**
- **1 teaspoon salt, divided**
- **½ teaspoon dried marjoram leaves, crushed**
- **¼ teaspoon pepper, divided**
- **½ cup soft fresh bread crumbs**
- **¼ cup grated Parmesan cheese**
- **1 pound ground beef**
- **1 can (14½ ounces) whole peeled tomatoes, undrained**
- **½ cup uncooked rotini or small macaroni**

1. To make stock, rinse bones. Combine bones, celery, carrots, onion and bay leaf in 6-quart stockpot or Dutch oven. Add water. Bring to a boil over high heat; reduce heat to low. Cover partially and simmer 1 hour, skimming foam occasionally.

2. Preheat oven to 400°F. Spray 13×9-inch baking pan with nonstick cooking spray. Combine egg, 3 tablespoons parsley, ½ teaspoon salt, marjoram and ⅛ teaspoon pepper in medium bowl; whisk lightly. Stir in bread crumbs and cheese. Add beef; mix well. Place meat mixture on cutting board; pat evenly into 1-inch-thick square. With sharp knife, cut meat into 1-inch squares; shape each square into a ball. Place meatballs in prepared pan; bake 20 to 25 minutes until brown on all sides and cooked through, turning occasionally. Drain on paper towels.

3. Strain stock through sieve into medium bowl. Slice celery and carrots; set aside. Discard bones, onion and bay leaf. To degrease stock, let stand 5 minutes to allow fat to rise. Holding paper towel, quickly pull across *surface only* of stock, allowing towel to absorb fat. Discard. Repeat with clean paper towels as many times as needed to remove all fat.

4. Return stock to stockpot. Drain tomatoes, reserving juice. Chop tomatoes; add to stock with juice. Bring to a boil over medium-high heat; uncover and boil 5 minutes. Stir in rotini, remaining ½ teaspoon salt and ⅛ teaspoon pepper. Cook 6 minutes, stirring occasionally. Add reserved vegetables and meatballs. Reduce heat to medium; cook 10 minutes until heated through. Stir in remaining 1 tablespoon parsley. Season to taste.

Makes 4 to 6 servings (about 7 cups)

Minestrone alla Milanese

- **1/4 pound green beans**
- **2 medium zucchini**
- **1 large potato**
- **1/2 pound cabbage**
- **1/3 cup olive oil**
- **3 tablespoons butter or margarine**
- **2 medium onions, chopped**
- **3 medium carrots, coarsely chopped**
- **3 ribs celery, coarsely chopped**
- **1 clove garlic, minced**
- **1 can (28 ounces) Italian plum tomatoes, undrained**
- **3 1/2 cups beef broth**
- **1 1/2 cups water**
- **1/2 teaspoon salt**
- **1/2 teaspoon dried basil leaves, crushed**
- **1/4 teaspoon dried rosemary leaves, crushed**
- **1/4 teaspoon pepper**
- **1 bay leaf**
- **1 can (16 ounces) cannellini beans**
- **Freshly grated Parmesan cheese (optional)**

1. Trim green beans; cut into 1-inch pieces. Trim zucchini; cut into 1/2-inch cubes. Peel potato; cut into 3/4-inch cubes. Coarsely shred cabbage.

2. Heat oil and butter in 6-quart stockpot or Dutch oven over medium heat. Add onions; cook and stir 6 to 8 minutes until onions are soft and golden but not brown. Stir in carrots and potato; cook and stir 5 minutes. Stir in celery and green beans; cook and stir 5 minutes. Stir in zucchini; cook and stir 3 minutes. Stir in cabbage and garlic; cook and stir 1 minute more.

3. Drain tomatoes, reserving juice. Add broth, water and reserved juice to stockpot. Chop tomatoes coarsely; add to stockpot. Stir in salt, basil, rosemary, pepper and bay leaf. Bring to a boil over high heat; reduce heat to low. Cover and simmer 1 1/2 hours, stirring occasionally.

4. Rinse and drain cannellini beans; add beans to stockpot.

Uncover and cook over medium-low heat 30 to 40 minutes more until soup thickens, stirring occasionally. Remove bay leaf. Serve with cheese.

Makes 8 to 10 servings (about 12 cups)

Spaghetti alla Bolognese

- **2 tablespoons olive oil**
- **1 medium onion, chopped**
- **1 pound ground beef**
- **½ small carrot, finely chopped**
- **½ rib celery, finely chopped**
- **1 cup dry white wine**
- **½ cup milk**
- **⅛ teaspoon ground nutmeg**
- **1 can (14½ ounces) whole peeled tomatoes, undrained**
- **1 cup beef broth**
- **3 tablespoons tomato paste**
- **1 teaspoon salt**
- **1 teaspoon dried basil leaves, crushed**
- **½ teaspoon dried thyme leaves, crushed**
- **⅛ teaspoon pepper**
- **1 bay leaf**
- **1 pound uncooked dry spaghetti**
- **1 cup freshly grated Parmesan cheese (about 3 ounces)**
- **Fresh thyme sprig for garnish**

1. Heat oil in large skillet over medium heat. Cook and stir onion in hot oil until soft. Crumble beef into onion mixture. Brown 6 minutes, stirring to separate meat, or until meat just loses its pink color.

2. Stir carrot and celery into meat mixture; cook 2 minutes over medium-high heat. Stir in wine; cook 4 to 6 minutes until wine has evaporated. Stir in milk and nutmeg; reduce heat to medium and cook 3 to 4 minutes until milk has evaporated Remove from heat.

3. Press tomatoes and juice through sieve into meat mixture; discard seeds.

4. Stir broth, tomato paste, salt, basil, dried thyme, pepper and bay leaf into tomato-meat mixture. Bring to a boil over medium-high heat; reduce heat to low. Simmer, uncovered, 1 to 1½ hours until most of liquid has evaporated and sauce thickens, stirring frequently. Remove and discard bay leaf.

5. To serve, cook spaghetti in large pot of boiling salted water 8 to 12 minutes just until al dente; drain well. Combine hot spaghetti and meat sauce in serving bowl; toss lightly. Sprinkle with cheese. Garnish, if desired.

Makes 4 to 6 servings

Fettuccine alla Carbonara

- **1 recipe Homemade Fettuccine (page 36) *or* ¾ pound uncooked dry fettuccine or spaghetti**
- **4 ounces pancetta (Italian bacon) or lean American bacon, cut into ½-inch-wide strips**
- **3 cloves garlic, halved**
- **¼ cup dry white wine**
- **⅓ cup heavy or whipping cream**
- **1 egg**
- **1 egg yolk**
- **⅔ cup freshly grated Parmesan cheese (about 2 ounces), divided**
- **Generous dash ground white pepper**
- **Fresh oregano leaves for garnish**

1. Prepare and cook Homemade Fettuccine or cook dry fettuccine in large pot of boiling salted water 6 to 8 minutes just until al dente; remove from heat. Drain well; return to dry pot.

2. Cook and stir pancetta and garlic in large skillet over medium-low heat 4 minutes or until pancetta is light brown. Reserve 2 tablespoons drippings in skillet with pancetta. Discard garlic and remaining drippings.

3. Add wine to pancetta mixture; cook over medium heat 3 minutes or until wine is almost evaporated. Stir in cream; cook and stir 2 minutes. Remove from heat.

4. Whisk egg and egg yolk in top of double boiler. Place top of double boiler over simmering water, adjusting heat to maintain simmer. Whisk ⅓ cup cheese and pepper into egg mixture; cook and stir until sauce thickens slightly.

5. Pour pancetta-cream mixture over fettuccine in pot; toss to coat. Heat over medium-low heat until heated through. Stir in egg-cheese mixture. Toss to coat evenly.

Remove from heat. Serve with remaining ⅓ cup cheese. Garnish, if desired.

Makes 4 servings

Four-Meat Ravioli

Four-Meat Filling (page 26)
Plum Tomato Sauce (page 26)
4 cups all-purpose flour
¼ teaspoon salt
2 eggs
1 tablespoon olive oil
⅔ to 1 cup water
1 egg yolk
1 teaspoon milk
1 tablespoon chopped fresh parsley
Freshly grated Parmesan cheese
Fresh rosemary sprig for garnish

1. Prepare Four-Meat Filling; refrigerate.

2. Prepare Plum Tomato Sauce; set aside.

3. For dough, mix flour and salt in large bowl. Combine 2 eggs, oil and ⅔ cup water in small bowl; whisk thoroughly. Gradually stir egg mixture into flour mixture with fork. Add enough of remaining ⅓ cup water, 1 tablespoon at a time, to form firm but pliable dough.

4. Place dough on lightly floured surface; flatten slightly. To knead dough, fold dough in half toward you and press dough away from you with heels of hands. Give dough a quarter turn and continue folding, pushing and turning. Continue kneading 5 minutes or until smooth and elastic, adding more flour to prevent sticking if necessary. Wrap dough in plastic wrap; let stand 30 minutes.

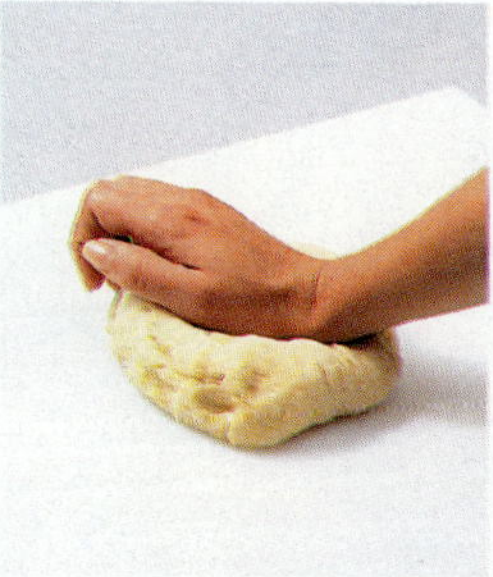

5. Unwrap dough and knead briefly (as described in step 4) on lightly floured surface; divide into 4 pieces. Using lightly floured rolling pin, roll out 1 dough piece to 1/16-inch thickness on lightly floured surface. (Keep remaining dough pieces wrapped in plastic wrap to prevent drying.) Cut dough into 4-inch-wide strips. Place teaspoonfuls of Four-Meat Filling along top half of each strip at 2-inch intervals.

continued on page 26

VIERGE

Four-Meat Ravioli, continued

6. Whisk egg yolk and milk in small bowl. Brush dough on long edge and between filling with egg-milk mixture. Fold dough over filling; press firmly between filling and along long edge to seal, making sure all air has been pushed out.

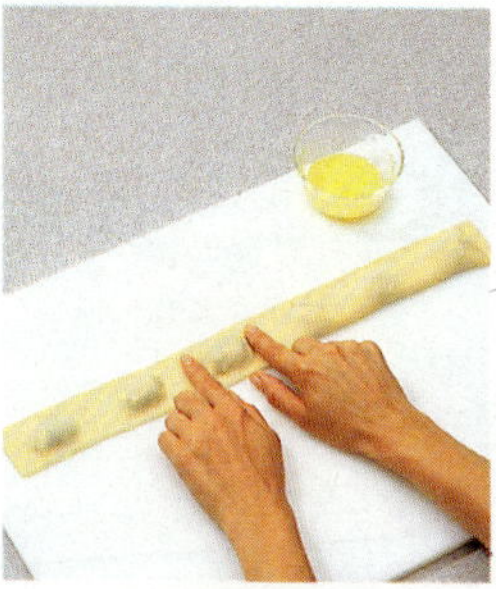

7. Cut ravioli apart with fluted pastry wheel. Repeat with remaining 3 dough pieces, filling and egg-milk mixture.

8. Cook ravioli, 1/4 at a time, in large pot of boiling salted water 3 to 5 minutes just until al dente. Remove with slotted spoon; drain well. Add ravioli to reserved sauce. Bring sauce and ravioli to a boil over medium-high heat; reduce heat to medium-low. Simmer, uncovered, 6 to 8 minutes until heated through. Sprinkle with parsley and cheese. Garnish, if desired. Serve immediately.

Makes 6 servings

Four-Meat Filling

5 ounces fresh spinach, cleaned, cooked (page 44, step 1) and squeezed dry
2 small boneless skinless chicken breast halves (about 4 ounces each), cooked
3 ounces prosciutto or cooked ham
1½ ounces hard salami
1 clove garlic
6 ounces ground beef
½ cup chopped fresh parsley
2 eggs
¼ teaspoon ground allspice
¼ teaspoon salt

Mince spinach, chicken, prosciutto, salami and garlic; combine in medium bowl with beef, parsley, eggs, allspice and salt. Mix well.

Plum Tomato Sauce

⅓ cup butter or margarine
1 clove garlic, minced
1 can (28 ounces) Italian plum tomatoes, undrained
1 can (8 ounces) tomato sauce
¾ teaspoon salt
½ teaspoon ground allspice
½ teaspoon dried basil leaves, crushed
½ teaspoon dried rosemary leaves, crushed
⅛ teaspoon pepper

1. Heat butter in large saucepan over medium heat until melted and bubbly; cook and stir garlic in hot butter 30 seconds. Press tomatoes and juice through sieve into garlic mixture; discard seeds. Stir in tomato sauce, salt, allspice, basil, rosemary and pepper.

2. Cover and simmer 30 minutes. Uncover and simmer 15 minutes more or until sauce thickens, stirring occasionally.

Chicken Tortellini with Mushroom-Cream Sauce

- **2 cups *plus* 1 tablespoon all-purpose flour**
- **½ teaspoon salt, divided**
- **4 eggs, divided**
- **1 tablespoon milk**
- **1 teaspoon olive oil**
- **2 small boneless skinless chicken breast halves (about 4 ounces each), cooked and minced**
- **2 ounces fresh spinach, cleaned, cooked (page 44, step 1), squeezed dry and minced**
- **2 ounces prosciutto or cooked ham, minced**
- **⅓ cup *plus* 2 tablespoons grated Parmesan cheese, divided**
- **2 cups heavy or whipping cream (1 pint), divided**
- **Dash pepper**
- **3 tablespoons butter or margarine**
- **½ pound fresh mushrooms, thinly sliced**
- **3 tablespoons chopped fresh parsley**

1. Combine flour and ¼ teaspoon salt on pastry board, cutting board or countertop; make well in center. Whisk 3 eggs, milk and oil in small bowl until well blended; gradually pour into well in flour mixture while mixing with fingertips or fork to form ball of dough.

2. Place dough on lightly floured surface; flatten slightly. To knead dough, fold dough in half toward you and press dough away from you with heels of hands. Give dough a quarter turn and continue folding, pushing and turning. Continue kneading 5 minutes or until smooth and elastic, adding more flour to prevent sticking if necessary. Wrap dough in plastic wrap; set aside. Allow dough to stand at least 15 minutes.

3. Combine chicken, spinach, prosciutto and remaining egg in medium bowl; mix well. Add 2 tablespoons cheese, 1 tablespoon cream, remaining ¼ teaspoon salt and pepper to spinach mixture; mix well.

continued on page 28

Chicken Tortellini with Mushroom-Cream Sauce, continued

4. Unwrap dough and knead briefly (as described in step 2) on lightly floured surface; divide into 3 pieces. Using lightly floured rolling pin, roll out 1 dough piece to 1/16-inch thickness on lightly floured surface. (Keep remaining dough pieces wrapped in plastic wrap to prevent drying.) Cut out dough circles with 2-inch round cutter. Cover rolled dough with clean kitchen towel to prevent drying while working.

5. Place ½ teaspoon chicken filling in center of 1 dough circle; brush edge of circle lightly with water.

Fold circle in half to enclose filling, making sure all air has been pushed out. Pinch outside edges together firmly to seal.

6. Brush end of half circle with water; wrap around finger overlapping ends. Pinch to seal. Place tortellini on clean kitchen towel. Repeat with remaining dough circles, rerolling dough scraps as needed. Repeat with remaining 2 dough pieces and chicken filling. Let tortellini dry on towel for 30 minutes before cooking.

7. Heat butter in 3-quart saucepan over medium heat until melted and bubbly; cook and stir mushrooms in hot butter 3 minutes. Stir in remaining cream. Bring to a boil over medium heat; immediately reduce heat to low. Simmer, uncovered, 3 minutes. Stir in remaining ⅓ cup cheese; cook and stir 1 minute. Remove from heat.

8. Cook tortellini, ⅓ at a time, in large pot of boiling salted water 2 to 3 minutes just until al dente. Drain well; add to mushroom-cream sauce. Bring mushroom-cream sauce and tortellini just to a boil over medium heat; reduce heat to low. Simmer 2 minutes. Sprinkle with parsley. Serve immediately.

Makes 6 to 8 servings

Spaghetti with Seafood Marinara Sauce

- **8 fresh oysters**
- **1 pound fresh medium shrimp**
- **1/2 pound fresh scallops**
- **6 flat anchovy fillets**
- **2 tablespoons olive oil**
- **1/3 cup chopped onion**
- **1 clove garlic, minced**
- **1/2 cup dry white wine**
- **10 ounces uncooked dry spaghetti**
- **5 large ripe tomatoes, seeded and chopped**
- **1 tablespoon tomato paste**
- **3/4 teaspoon dried basil, crumbled**
- **3/4 teaspoon salt**
- **1/2 teaspoon dried oregano, crumbled**
- **1/8 teaspoon pepper**
- **3 tablespoons chopped fresh parsley**
- **Fresh basil leaves for garnish**

1. Scrub oysters thoroughly with stiff brush under cold running water. Place on tray and refrigerate 1 hour to help oysters relax. To shuck oysters, take pointed oyster knife in one hand and thick towel or glove in the other. With towel, grip shell in palm of hand. Keeping oyster level with knife, insert tip of knife between the shell next to hinge; twist to pry shell until you hear a snap. (Use knife as leverage; do not force.)

2. Twist to open shell, keeping oyster level at all times to save liquor. Cut the muscle from shell and discard top shell.

Tip shell over strainer in bowl to catch oysters; discard bottom shell. Refrigerate oysters. Strain oyster liquor from bowl through triple thickness of dampened cheesecloth into small bowl; set aside oyster liquor.

continued on page 32

Spaghetti with Seafood Marinara Sauce, continued

3. Remove shells from shrimp under cold running water. To devein, cut shallow slit down back of shrimp; pull out and discard vein (technique on page 14). Cut scallops into 3/4-inch pieces. Drain and mince anchovies. Refrigerate seafood.

4. Heat oil in 3-quart saucepan over medium-high heat; cook and stir onion in hot oil 4 minutes or until soft. Add garlic; cook 30 seconds. Add wine; cook 4 to 5 minutes until wine has evaporated. Remove from heat; cover and set aside.

5. Cook spaghetti in large pot of boiling salted water 8 to 10 minutes just until al dente; drain well.

6. Stir reserved oyster liquor and anchovies into reserved onion mixture in saucepan; add tomatoes, tomato paste, basil, salt, oregano and pepper. Mix well. Bring to a boil over high heat; reduce heat to medium. Cook, uncovered, 20 minutes or until sauce thickens, stirring occasionally.

7. Stir in reserved shrimp, scallops and oysters. Cover and cook 2 to 3 minutes until shrimp turn opaque and are cooked through, stirring occasionally. Stir in parsley.

8. Combine hot spaghetti with seafood sauce in large serving bowl; toss until well coated. Garnish, if desired. Serve immediately.

Makes 4 to 5 servings

Spinach Lasagna

- **1 pound ground beef**
- **¼ pound fresh mushrooms, thinly sliced**
- **1 medium onion, chopped**
- **1 clove garlic, minced**
- **1 can (28 ounces) Italian plum tomatoes, undrained**
- **1¼ teaspoons salt, divided**
- **¾ teaspoon dried oregano leaves, crushed**
- **¾ teaspoon dried basil leaves, crushed**
- **¼ teaspoon pepper, divided**
- **9 uncooked lasagna noodles**
- **¼ cup *plus* 1 tablespoon butter or margarine, divided**
- **¼ cup all-purpose flour**
- **⅛ teaspoon ground nutmeg**
- **2 cups milk**
- **1½ cups shredded mozzarella cheese (about 6 ounces), divided**
- **½ cup freshly grated Parmesan cheese, divided**
- **1 package (10 ounces) frozen chopped spinach, thawed and squeezed dry**

1. For meat sauce, crumble ground beef into large skillet over medium-high heat. Brown 8 to 10 minutes, stirring to separate meat, until meat loses its pink color. Stir in mushrooms, onion and garlic; cook over medium heat 5 minutes or until onion is soft.

2. Press tomatoes and juice through sieve into meat mixture; discard seeds. Stir in ¾ teaspoon salt, oregano, basil and ⅛ teaspoon pepper. Bring to a boil over medium-high heat; reduce heat to low. Cover and simmer 40 minutes, stirring occasionally. Uncover and simmer 15 to 20 minutes more until sauce thickens. Set aside.

3. Add lasagna noodles to large pot of boiling salted water, 1 at a time, allowing noodles to soften and fit into pot. Cook 10 minutes or just until al dente. Drain noodles; rinse with cold water. Drain again; hang individually over pot rim to prevent sticking. Set aside.

4. For cheese sauce, melt ¼ cup butter in medium saucepan over medium heat. Stir in flour, remaining ½ teaspoon salt, remaining ⅛ teaspoon pepper and nutmeg; cook and stir until bubbly. Whisk in milk; cook and stir until sauce thickens and bubbles. Cook and stir 1 minute more. Remove from heat. Stir in 1 cup mozzarella and ¼ cup Parmesan cheeses. Stir until smooth. Set aside.

continued on page 34

Spinach Lasagna, continued

5. Preheat oven to 350°F. Spread remaining 1 tablespoon butter on bottom and sides of 12×8-inch baking dish with waxed paper. Spread noodles in single layer on clean kitchen (not paper) towel. Pat noodles dry.

6. Arrange 3 lasagna noodles in single layer, overlapping slightly, in bottom of baking dish. Top with 1/2 of reserved meat sauce; spread evenly. Spread 1/2 of reserved cheese sauce over meat sauce in even layer.

7. Repeat layers once, using 3 noodles, remaining meat sauce and remaining cheese sauce. Sprinkle spinach over cheese sauce in even layer; pat down lightly. Arrange remaining 3 lasagna noodles over spinach.

8. Mix remaining 1/2 cup mozzarella and 1/4 cup Parmesan cheeses in cup. Sprinkle cheeses evenly on top of

lasagna to completely cover lasagna noodles. Bake 40 minutes or until top is golden and edges are bubbly. Let lasagna stand 10 minutes before serving. Garnish as desired.

Makes 6 servings

Classic Fettuccine Alfredo

1 recipe Homemade Fettuccine (recipe follows) *or* ¾ pound uncooked dry fettuccine
6 tablespoons unsalted butter
⅔ cup heavy or whipping cream
½ teaspoon salt
Generous dash ground white pepper
Generous dash ground nutmeg
1 cup freshly grated Parmesan cheese (about 3 ounces)
2 tablespoons chopped fresh parsley
Fresh Italian parsley sprig for garnish

1. Prepare and cook Homemade Fettuccine or cook dry fettuccine in large pot of boiling salted water 6 to 8 minutes just until al dente; remove from heat. Drain well; return to dry pot.

2. Place butter and cream in large, heavy skillet over medium-low heat. Cook and stir until butter melts and mixture bubbles. Cook and stir 2 minutes more. Stir in salt, pepper and nutmeg. Remove from heat. Gradually stir in cheese until thoroughly blended and smooth. Return briefly to heat to completely blend cheese if necessary. (Do not let sauce bubble or cheese will become lumpy and tough.)

3. Pour sauce over fettuccine in pot. Stir and toss with 2 forks over low heat 2 to 3 minutes until sauce is thickened and fettuccine is evenly coated. Sprinkle with parsley. Garnish, if desired. Serve immediately.

Makes 4 servings

Homemade Fettuccine

2 cups all-purpose flour
¼ teaspoon salt
3 eggs
1 tablespoon milk
1 teaspoon olive oil

1. Combine flour and salt on pastry board, cutting board or countertop; make well in center. Whisk eggs, milk and oil in small bowl until well blended; gradually pour into well in flour mixture while mixing with fork or fingertips to form ball of dough.

2. Place dough on lightly floured surface; flatten slightly. To knead dough, fold dough in half toward you and press dough away from you with heels of hands. Give dough a quarter turn and continue folding, pushing and turning.

continued on page 38

Classic Fettuccine Alfredo, continued

Continue kneading 5 minutes or until smooth and elastic, adding more flour to prevent sticking if necessary. Wrap dough in plastic wrap; let stand 15 minutes.

3. Unwrap dough and knead briefly (as described in step 2) on lightly floured surface. Using lightly floured rolling pin, roll out dough to 1/8-inch-thick circle on lightly floured surface. Gently pick up dough circle with both hands. Hold it up to the light to check for places where dough is too thick.

Return to board; even out any thick spots. Let rest until dough is slightly dry but can be handled without breaking.

4. Lightly flour dough circle; roll loosely on rolling pin.

Slide rolling pin out; press dough roll gently with hand and cut into 1/4-inch-wide strips with sharp knife. Carefully unfold strips.*

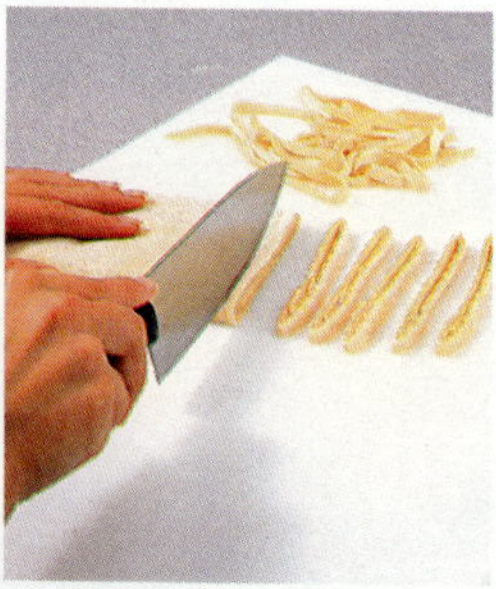

5. Cook fettuccine in large pot of boiling salted water 1 to 2 minutes just until al dente. Drain well.

Makes about 3/4 pound

*Fettuccine can be dried and stored at this point. Hang fettuccine strips over pasta rack or clean broom handle covered with plastic wrap and propped between two chairs. Dry at least 3 hours; store in airtight container at room temperature up to 4 days. To serve, cook fettuccine in large pot of boiling salted water 3 to 4 minutes just until al dente. Drain well.

Homemade Angel Hair Pasta with Classic Tomato Sauces

- **2 cups *plus* 2 tablespoons all-purpose flour**
- **¼ teaspoon salt**
- **3 eggs**
- **1 tablespoon milk**
- **1 teaspoon olive oil**
- **Neapolitan Sauce (page 40)**
- **Pizzaiola Sauce (page 40)**
- **½ cup freshly grated Parmesan cheese (optional)**
- **Fresh marjoram sprigs for garnish**

1. Place flour, salt, eggs, milk and oil in food processor; process until dough forms. Shape into ball.

2. Place dough on lightly floured surface; flatten slightly. Cut dough into 4 pieces. Wrap 3 dough pieces in plastic wrap; set aside.

3. To knead dough by pasta machine,* set rollers of pasta machine at widest setting (position 1). Feed unwrapped dough piece through flat rollers by turning handle. (Dough may crumble slightly at first but will hold together after two to three rollings.)

4. Lightly flour dough strip; fold strip into thirds. Feed through rollers again. Continue process 7 to 10 times until dough is smooth and elastic.

5. To roll out dough by machine, reduce setting to position 3. Feed dough strip through rollers. Without folding strip into thirds, repeat on positions 5 and 6. Let dough stand 5 to 10 minutes until slightly dry.

6. Attach handle to angel hair pasta roller and feed dough through, catching angel hair pasta with free hand as it emerges.** Repeat kneading and rolling with reserved dough pieces.

7. Cook angel hair pasta in large pot of boiling salted water 1 to 2 minutes just until al dente; remove from heat. Drain well; divide angel hair pasta into 2 large bowls.

continued on page 40

Homemade Angel Hair Pasta with Classic Tomato Sauces, continued

8. Prepare Neapolitan Sauce and Pizzaiola Sauce.

9. Pour hot Neapolitan Sauce over 1/2 of angel hair pasta; toss until well coated. Pour hot Pizzaiola Sauce over remaining angel hair pasta; toss until well coated. Serve with cheese. Garnish, if desired.

Makes 4 to 6 servings

*Follow manufacturer's directions for appropriate method of rolling pasta if position settings are different. To make pasta by hand, see Homemade Fettuccine (page 36).

**Angel hair pasta can be dried and stored at this point. Hang pasta strips over pasta rack or clean broom handle covered with plastic wrap and propped between two chairs. (Or, twirl pasta into nests and place on clean kitchen towel.) Dry at least 3 hours; store in airtight container at room temperature up to 4 days. To serve, cook angel hair pasta in large pot of boiling salted water 3 to 4 minutes just until al dente. Drain well; proceed as directed in step 8.

Neapolitan Sauce

- **2 tablespoons butter or margarine**
- **1 tablespoon olive oil**
- **1 can (28 ounces) Italian plum tomatoes, undrained**
- **1 teaspoon dried basil leaves, crushed**
- **1/2 teaspoon salt**
- **1/8 teaspoon pepper**
- **3 tablespoons chopped fresh parsley**

Heat butter and oil in 2-quart saucepan over medium heat. Press tomatoes and juice through sieve into hot butter mixture; discard seeds. Stir in basil, salt and pepper. Bring to a boil over high heat; reduce heat to medium-low. Cook, uncovered, 30 to 40 minutes until sauce is reduced to 2 cups, stirring frequently. Stir in parsley.

Pizzaiola Sauce

- **1 tablespoon olive oil**
- **2 cloves garlic**
- **1 can (28 ounces) Italian plum tomatoes, undrained**
- **3/4 teaspoon dried marjoram leaves, crushed**
- **1/2 teaspoon salt**
- **1/8 teaspoon pepper**
- **2 tablespoons minced fresh parsley**

Heat oil in 2-quart saucepan over medium heat. Cut garlic in half. Cook and stir garlic in hot oil 2 to 3 minutes until garlic is golden but not brown. Remove and discard garlic. Press tomatoes and juice through sieve into garlic-flavored oil; discard seeds. Stir in marjoram, salt and pepper. Bring to a boil over high heat; reduce heat to medium-low. Cook, uncovered, 30 to 40 minutes until sauce is reduced to 2 cups, stirring frequently. Stir in parsley.

Classic Pesto with Linguine

Homemade Linguine *or* 3/4 pound dry uncooked linguine, hot cooked and drained
2 tablespoons butter or margarine
1/4 cup *plus* 1 tablespoon olive oil, divided
2 tablespoons pine nuts
1 cup tightly packed fresh basil leaves, rinsed, drained and stemmed (do not use dried basil)
2 cloves garlic
1/4 teaspoon salt
1/4 cup freshly grated Parmesan cheese
1 1/2 tablespoons freshly grated Romano cheese
Fresh basil leaves for garnish

1. To prepare Homemade Linguine, make dough following steps 1 and 2 of Homemade Fettuccine (page 36). In step 3, roll out dough to 1/16-inch-thick circle. In step 4, cut dough into 1/8-inch-wide strips. Proceed as directed in step 5. Add butter to cooked and drained pasta, tossing to coat evenly.

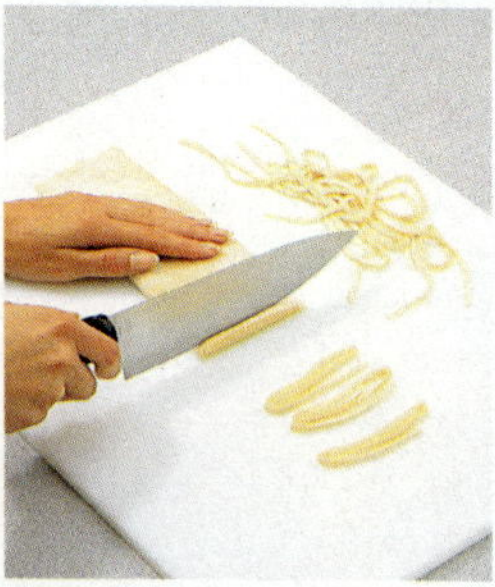

2. To toast pine nuts, heat 1 tablespoon oil in small saucepan or skillet over medium-low heat. Add pine nuts; cook and stir 30 to 45 seconds until light brown, shaking pan constantly. Remove with slotted spoon; drain on paper towels.

3. Place toasted pine nuts, basil leaves, garlic and salt in food processor or blender. With processor running, add remaining 1/4 cup oil in slow steady stream until evenly blended and pine nuts are finely chopped.

4. Transfer basil mixture to small bowl. Stir in Parmesan and Romano cheeses.*

5. Combine hot, buttered linguine and pesto sauce in large serving bowl; toss until well coated. Garnish, if desired. Serve immediately.

Makes 4 servings (about 3/4 cup pesto)

*Pesto sauce can be stored at this point in airtight container; pour thin layer of olive oil over pesto and cover. Refrigerate up to 1 week. Bring to room temperature. Proceed as directed in step 5.

Classic Veal Florentine

6 ounces fresh spinach
6 tablespoons butter or margarine, divided
2 cloves garlic, minced
1 can (14½ ounces) whole peeled tomatoes, undrained
¼ cup dry white wine
¼ cup water
1 tablespoon tomato paste
½ teaspoon sugar
¾ teaspoon salt, divided
¼ teaspoon pepper, divided
¼ cup all-purpose flour
4 veal cutlets, cut ⅜ inch thick (about 4 ounces each)
1 tablespoon olive oil
4 ounces mozzarella cheese, shredded
Homemade Angel Hair Pasta (page 39) (optional)

1. To steam spinach, rinse spinach thoroughly in large bowl of water; drain but do not squeeze dry. Trim and discard stems. Stack leaves; cut crosswise into coarse shreds. Place spinach in large saucepan over medium heat. Cover and steam 4 minutes or until tender, stirring occasionally. Add 2 tablespoons butter; cook and stir until butter is absorbed. Remove from pan; set aside.

2. To make tomato sauce, heat 2 tablespoons butter in medium saucepan over medium heat until melted and bubbly. Add garlic; cook and stir 30 seconds. Press tomatoes and juice through sieve into garlic mixture; discard seeds. Add wine, water, tomato paste, sugar, ½ teaspoon salt and ⅛ teaspoon pepper to tomato mixture. Bring to a boil; reduce heat to low. Simmer, uncovered, 10 minutes, stirring occasionally. Remove from heat; set aside.

3. Mix flour, remaining ¼ teaspoon salt and ⅛ teaspoon pepper in small plastic bag. Pound veal with meat mallet to ¼-inch thickness (technique on page 46). Pat dry with paper towels. Shake veal, 1 cutlet at a time, in seasoned flour to coat evenly.

4. Heat oil and remaining 2 tablespoons butter in large skillet over medium heat until bubbly. Add veal to skillet; cook 2 to 3 minutes per side until light brown. Remove from heat. Spoon off excess fat. Top veal with reserved spinach, then cheese.

5. Pour reserved tomato mixture into skillet, lifting edges of veal to let sauce flow under.

Cook over low heat until bubbly. Cover and simmer 8 minutes or until heated through. Serve with pasta. Garnish as desired.

Makes 4 servings

Veal Scallopine

4 veal cutlets, cut 3/8 inch thick (about 4 ounces each)
1/4 cup butter or margarine
1/2 pound fresh mushrooms, thinly sliced
2 tablespoons olive oil
1 small onion, finely chopped
1/4 cup dry sherry
2 teaspoons all-purpose flour
1/2 cup beef broth
1/4 teaspoon salt
1/8 teaspoon pepper
2 tablespoons heavy or whipping cream
Fresh bay leaf and marjoram sprigs for garnish
Hot cooked pasta (optional)

1. Place each veal cutlet between sheets of waxed paper on cutting board. Pound veal with meat mallet to 1/4-inch thickness. Pat dry with paper towels; set aside.

2. Heat butter in large skillet over medium heat until melted and bubbly. Cook and stir mushrooms in hot butter 3 to 4 minutes until light brown. Remove mushrooms with slotted spoon to small bowl; set aside.

3. Add oil to butter remaining in skillet; heat over medium heat. Add veal; cook 2 to 3 minutes per side until light brown. Remove veal with slotted spatula to plate; set aside.

4. Add onion to same skillet; cook and stir 2 to 3 minutes until soft. Stir sherry into onion mixture. Bring to a boil over medium-high heat; boil 15 seconds. Stir in flour; cook and stir 30 seconds. Remove from heat; stir in broth. Bring to a boil over medium heat, stirring constantly. Stir in reserved mushrooms, salt and pepper. Add reserved veal to sauce mixture; reduce heat to low. Cover and simmer 8 minutes or until veal is tender. Remove from heat.

5. Push veal to one side of skillet. Stir cream into sauce mixture; mix well.

Cook over low heat until heated through. Garnish, if desired. Serve immediately with pasta.

Makes 4 servings

Veal Parmesan

4 veal cutlets, cut 3/8 inch thick (about 4 ounces each)
4 tablespoons olive oil, divided
1 small red bell pepper, finely chopped
1 medium onion, finely chopped
1 rib celery, finely chopped
1 clove garlic, minced
1 can (14½ ounces) whole peeled tomatoes, undrained and finely chopped
1 cup chicken broth
1 tablespoon tomato paste
1 tablespoon chopped parsley
1 teaspoon sugar
¾ teaspoon dried basil leaves, crushed
½ teaspoon salt
⅛ teaspoon ground black pepper
1 egg
¼ cup all-purpose flour
⅔ cup fine dry bread crumbs
2 tablespoons butter
1½ cups shredded mozzarella cheese (about 6 ounces)
⅔ cup freshly grated Parmesan cheese
Fresh basil leaves for garnish
Hot cooked pasta

1. Pound veal with meat mallet to ¼-inch thickness (technique on page 46). Pat dry with paper towels; set aside.

2. To make tomato sauce, heat 1 tablespoon oil in medium saucepan over medium heat. Cook and stir bell pepper, onion, celery and garlic in hot oil 5 minutes. Stir in tomatoes and juice, broth, tomato paste, parsley, sugar, dried basil, salt and black pepper. Cover and simmer over low heat 20 minutes. Uncover and cook over medium heat 20 minutes more or until sauce thickens, stirring frequently; set aside.

3. Beat egg in shallow bowl; spread flour and bread crumbs on separate plates. Dip reserved veal cutlets to coat both sides evenly, first in flour, then in egg, then in bread crumbs. Press crumb coating firmly onto veal.

4. Heat butter and 2 tablespoons oil in large skillet over medium-high heat. Add veal. Cook 3 minutes per side or until browned.

5. Preheat oven to 350°F. Remove veal with slotted spatula to ungreased 13×9-inch baking dish. Sprinkle mozzarella cheese evenly over veal. Spoon reserved tomato sauce evenly over cheese. Sprinkle Parmesan cheese over tomato sauce.

6. Drizzle remaining 1 tablespoon oil over top. Bake, uncovered, 25 minutes or until veal is tender and cheese is golden. Garnish, if desired. Serve with pasta.

Makes 4 servings

Chicken Cacciatore

- **1 broiler-fryer chicken (3 to 3½ pounds), cut into 8 pieces**
- **1 tablespoon olive oil**
- **4 ounces fresh mushrooms, finely chopped**
- **1 medium onion, chopped**
- **1 clove garlic, minced**
- **½ cup dry white wine**
- **1½ tablespoons white wine vinegar**
- **½ cup chicken broth**
- **1 teaspoon dried basil leaves, crushed**
- **½ teaspoon dried marjoram leaves, crushed**
- **½ teaspoon salt**
- **⅛ teaspoon pepper**
- **1 can (14½ ounces) whole peeled tomatoes, undrained**
- **8 Italian- or Greek-style black olives**
- **1 tablespoon chopped fresh parsley**
- **Hot cooked pasta**
- **Fresh marjoram leaves for garnish**

1. Rinse chicken; drain and pat dry with paper towels. Heat oil in large skillet over medium heat. Add as many chicken pieces in single layer without crowding to hot oil. Cook 8 minutes per side or until chicken is brown; remove chicken with slotted spatula to Dutch oven. Repeat with remaining chicken pieces.

2. Add mushrooms and onion to drippings remaining in skillet. Cook and stir over medium heat 5 minutes or until onion is soft. Add garlic; cook and stir 30 seconds. Add wine and vinegar; cook over medium-high heat 5 minutes or until liquid is almost evaporated. Stir in broth, basil, marjoram, salt and pepper. Remove from heat.

3. Press tomatoes and juice through sieve into onion mixture; discard seeds. Bring to a boil over medium-high heat; boil, uncovered, 2 minutes.

4. Pour tomato-onion mixture over chicken. Bring to a boil; reduce heat to low. Cover and simmer 25 minutes or until chicken is tender and juices run clear when pierced with fork. Remove chicken with slotted spatula to heated serving dish; keep warm.

5. Bring tomato-onion sauce to a boil over medium-high heat; boil, uncovered, 5 minutes. Cut olives in half; remove and discard pits.

6. Add olives and parsley to sauce; cook 1 minute more. Pour sauce over chicken and pasta. Garnish, if desired.

Makes 4 to 6 servings

Classic Chicken Marsala

- **2 tablespoons unsalted butter**
- **1 tablespoon vegetable oil**
- **4 boneless skinless chicken breast halves (about 1¼ pounds total)**
- **4 slices mozzarella cheese (1 ounce each)**
- **12 capers, drained**
- **4 flat anchovy fillets, drained**
- **1 tablespoon chopped fresh parsley**
- **1 clove garlic, minced**
- **3 tablespoons marsala**
- **⅔ cup heavy or whipping cream**
- **Dash salt**
- **Dash pepper**
- **Hot cooked pasta (optional)**

1. Heat butter and oil in large skillet over medium-high heat until melted and bubbly. Add chicken; reduce heat to medium. Cook, uncovered, 5 to 6 minutes per side until chicken is tender and golden brown. Remove chicken with slotted spatula to work surface. Top each chicken piece with 1 cheese slice, 3 capers and 1 anchovy fillet.

2. Return chicken to skillet. Sprinkle with parsley. Cover and cook over low heat 3 minutes or until cheese is semi-melted and juices from chicken run clear. Remove chicken with slotted spatula to heated serving dish; keep warm.

3. Add garlic to drippings remaining in skillet; cook and stir over medium heat 30 seconds. Stir in marsala; cook and stir 45 seconds, scraping up any brown bits in skillet.

4. Stir in cream. Cook and stir 3 minutes or until sauce thickens slightly. Stir in salt and pepper. Spoon sauce over chicken. Serve with pasta. Garnish as desired.

Makes 4 servings

Fish alla Milanese

- **1/3 cup *plus* 2 tablespoons olive oil, divided**
- **2 tablespoons lemon juice**
- **1/2 teaspoon salt**
- **Dash pepper**
- **1 small onion, finely chopped**
- **1 pound flounder or haddock fillets (4 to 8 pieces)**
- **2 eggs**
- **1 tablespoon milk**
- **1/2 cup all-purpose flour**
- **3/4 cup fine dry unseasoned bread crumbs**
- **1/4 cup *plus* 2 tablespoons butter or margarine, divided**
- **1 clove garlic, minced**
- **1 tablespoon chopped fresh parsley**
- **Fresh thyme sprig for garnish**
- **Lemon slices (optional)**

1. For marinade, whisk 1/3 cup oil, lemon juice, salt and pepper in small bowl; stir in onion. Pour marinade into 13×9-inch glass baking dish.

2. Rinse fish; pat dry with paper towels. Place fish in baking dish; spoon marinade over fish to coat thoroughly. Marinate, covered, in refrigerator 1 hour, turning fish over occasionally.

3. Combine eggs and milk in shallow bowl; mix well. Spread flour and bread crumbs on separate plates. Remove fish from marinade; pat dry with paper towels. Discard marinade.

4. Dip fish to coat both sides evenly, first in flour, then in egg mixture, then in bread crumbs. Press crumb coating firmly onto fish. Place on waxed paper; refrigerate 15 minutes.

5. Heat remaining 2 tablespoons oil and 2 tablespoons butter in large skillet over medium heat until melted and bubbly; add fish. Cook 2 to 3 minutes per side until fish flakes easily with a fork and topping is light brown. Remove to heated serving plate.

6. Melt remaining 1/4 cup butter in medium skillet over medium heat. Add garlic. Cook 1 to 2 minutes until butter turns light brown; stir in parsley. Pour browned butter mixture over fish. Garnish, if desired. Serve immediately with lemon slices.

Makes 4 servings

Fried Calamari with Tartar Sauce

1 pound fresh or thawed frozen squid
1 egg
1 tablespoon milk
¾ cup fine dry unseasoned bread crumbs
Vegetable oil
Tartar Sauce (page 58)
Lemon wedges (optional)

1. To clean each squid, hold body of squid firmly in one hand. Grasp head firmly with other hand; pull head, twisting gently from side to side. (Head and contents of body should pull away in one piece.) Set aside tubular body sac. Cut tentacles off head; set aside. Discard head and contents of body.

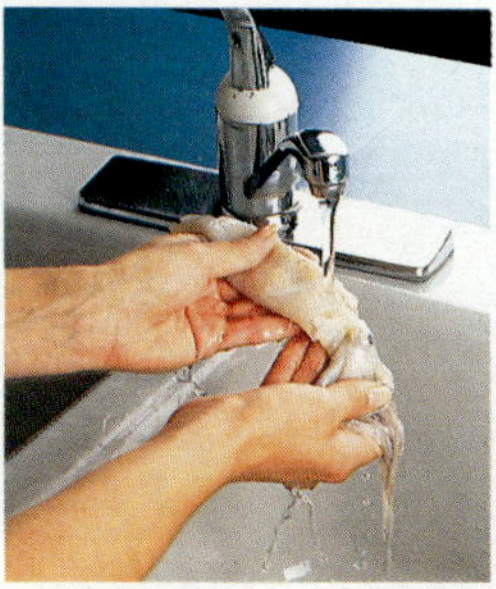

2. Grasp tip of pointed, thin, clear cartilage protruding from body; pull out and discard. Rinse squid under cold running water. Peel off and discard spotted outer membrane covering body sac and fins. Pull off side fins; set aside. Rinse inside of squid body thoroughly under running water. Repeat with remaining squid.

3. Cut each squid body crosswise into ¼-inch rings. Cut reserved fins into thin slices. (Body rings, fins and reserved tentacles are all edible parts.) Pat pieces thoroughly dry with paper towels.

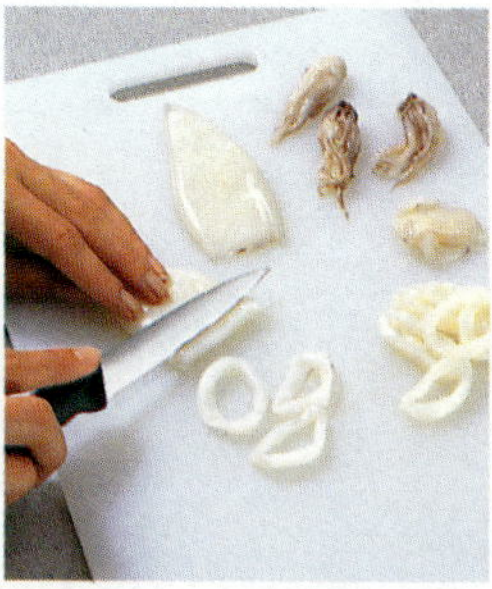

4. Beat egg with milk in small bowl. Add squid pieces; stir to coat well. Spread bread crumbs on plate. Dip squid pieces in bread crumbs; place in shallow bowl or on waxed paper. Let stand 10 to 15 minutes before frying.

continued on page 58

Fried Calamari with Tartar Sauce, continued

5. To deep fry squid,* heat 1½ inches oil in large saucepan to 350°F. (*Caution:* Squid will pop and spatter during frying; do not stand too close to pan.) Adjust heat to maintain temperature. Fry 8 to 10 pieces of squid at a time in hot oil 45 to 60 seconds until light brown. Remove with slotted spoon; drain on paper towels. Repeat with remaining squid pieces.

6. Serve hot with Tartar Sauce and lemon wedges. Garnish as desired.

Makes 2 to 3 servings

*To shallow fry squid, heat about ¼ inch oil in large skillet over medium-high heat; reduce heat to medium. Add as many pieces of squid in single layer without crowding to hot oil. Cook, turning once with 2 forks, 1 minute per side or until light brown. Proceed as directed in step 5. (This method uses less oil but requires slightly more hand work.)

Tartar Sauce

1 green onion
1 tablespoon drained capers
1 small sweet gherkin or pickle
2 tablespoons chopped fresh parsley
1⅓ cups mayonnaise

1. Thinly slice green onion. Mince capers and gherkin.

2. Fold green onion, capers, gherkin and parsley into mayonnaise. Cover and refrigerate until ready to serve.

Makes about 1⅓ cups

Homemade Pizza

- **½ tablespoon active dry yeast**
- **1 teaspoon sugar, divided**
- **½ cup warm water (105°F to 115°F)**
- **1¾ cups all-purpose flour, divided**
- **¾ teaspoon salt, divided**
- **2 tablespoons olive oil, divided**
- **1 can (14½ ounces) whole peeled tomatoes, undrained**
- **1 medium onion, chopped**
- **1 clove garlic, minced**
- **2 tablespoons tomato paste**
- **1 teaspoon dried oregano leaves, crushed**
- **½ teaspoon dried basil leaves, crushed**
- **⅛ teaspoon ground black pepper**
- **½ small red bell pepper, cored and seeded**
- **½ small green bell pepper, cored and seeded**
- **4 fresh medium mushrooms**
- **1 can (2 ounces) flat anchovy fillets**
- **1¾ cups shredded mozzarella cheese**
- **½ cup freshly grated Parmesan cheese**
- **⅓ cup pitted ripe olives, halved**

1. To proof yeast, sprinkle yeast and ½ teaspoon sugar over warm water in small bowl; stir until yeast is dissolved. Let stand 5 minutes or until mixture is bubbly.*

2. Place 1½ cups flour and ¼ teaspoon salt in medium bowl; stir in yeast mixture and 1 tablespoon oil, stirring until a smooth, soft dough forms. Place dough on lightly floured surface; flatten slightly. To knead dough, fold dough in half toward you and press dough away from you with heels of hands. Give dough a quarter turn and continue folding, pushing and turning. Continue kneading, using as much of remaining flour as needed to form a stiff, elastic dough.

3. Shape dough into a ball; place in large greased bowl. Turn to grease entire surface. Cover with clean kitchen towel and let dough rise in warm place 30 to 45 minutes until doubled in bulk. Press two fingertips about ½ inch into dough. Dough is ready if indentations remain when fingers are removed.

continued on page 60

Homemade Pizza, continued

4. For sauce, finely chop tomatoes in can with knife, reserving juice. Heat remaining 1 tablespoon oil in medium saucepan over medium heat. Add onion; cook 5 minutes or until soft. Add garlic; cook 30 seconds more. Add tomatoes and juice, tomato paste, oregano, basil, remaining ½ teaspoon sugar, ½ teaspoon salt and black pepper. Bring to a boil over high heat; reduce heat to medium-low. Simmer, uncovered, 10 to 15 minutes until sauce thickens, stirring occasionally. Pour into small bowl; cool.

5. Punch dough down. Knead briefly (as described in step 2) on lightly floured surface to distribute air bubbles; let dough stand 5 minutes more. Flatten dough into circle on lightly floured surface. Roll out dough, starting at center and rolling to edges, into 10-inch circle. Place circle in greased 12-inch pizza pan; stretch and pat dough out to edges of pan. Cover and let stand 15 minutes.

6. Preheat oven to 450°F. Cut bell peppers into ¾-inch pieces. Trim mushroom stems; wipe clean with damp kitchen towel (technique on page 12) and thinly slice. Drain anchovies. Mix mozzarella and Parmesan cheeses in small bowl. Spread sauce evenly over pizza dough.

Sprinkle with ⅔ of cheeses. Arrange bell peppers, mushrooms, anchovies and olives over cheeses.

7. Sprinkle remaining cheeses on top of pizza. Bake 20 minutes or until crust is golden brown. To serve, cut into wedges.

Makes 4 to 6 servings

*If yeast does not bubble, it is no longer active. Always check expiration date on yeast packet. Also, water that is too hot will kill yeast; it is best to use a thermometer.

Tomato, Mozzarella & Basil Salad

2 tablespoons red wine vinegar
1 clove garlic, minced
½ teaspoon salt
¼ teaspoon dry mustard
Generous dash freshly ground black pepper
⅓ cup olive or vegetable oil
4 Italian plum tomatoes
6 ounces mozzarella cheese
8 to 10 fresh basil leaves

1. For dressing, combine vinegar, garlic, salt, mustard and pepper in small bowl. Add oil in slow steady stream, whisking until oil is thoroughly blended.

2. Slice tomatoes and cheese into ¼-inch-thick slices. Trim cheese slices to size of tomato slices.

3. Place tomato and cheese slices in large, shallow bowl or glass baking dish. Pour dressing over slices; Marinate, covered, in refrigerator at least 30 minutes or up to 3 hours, turning slices occasionally.

4. Layer basil leaves with largest leaf on bottom, then roll up jelly-roll fashion. Slice basil roll into ¼-inch-thick slices; separate into strips.

5. Arrange tomato and cheese slices alternately on serving plate or 4 individual salad plates. Sprinkle with basil strips; drizzle with remaining dressing.

Makes 4 servings

Fennel, Olive and Radicchio Salad

11 Italian- or Greek-style black olives, divided
¼ cup olive oil
1 tablespoon lemon juice
1 flat anchovy fillet *or* ½ teaspoon anchovy paste
¼ teaspoon salt
Generous dash freshly ground black pepper
Generous dash sugar
1 fresh fennel bulb
1 head radicchio*
Fennel greenery for garnish

*Radicchio, a tart red chicory, is available in large supermarkets and specialty food shops. If not available, 2 heads of Belgian endive can be used; although it does not provide the dramatic red color, it will give a similar texture and its slightly bitter flavor will go well with the robust dressing and the sweet anise flavor of fennel.

1. For dressing, cut 3 olives in half; remove and discard pits (technique on page 50). Place pitted olives, oil, lemon juice and anchovy in food processor or blender; process 5 seconds. Add salt, pepper and sugar; process until olives are finely chopped, about 5 seconds more. Set aside.

2. Cut off and discard fennel stalks. Cut off and discard root end at base of fennel bulb and any discolored parts of bulb. Cut fennel bulb lengthwise into 8 wedges; separate each wedge into segments.

3. Separate radicchio leaves; rinse thoroughly under running water. Drain well.

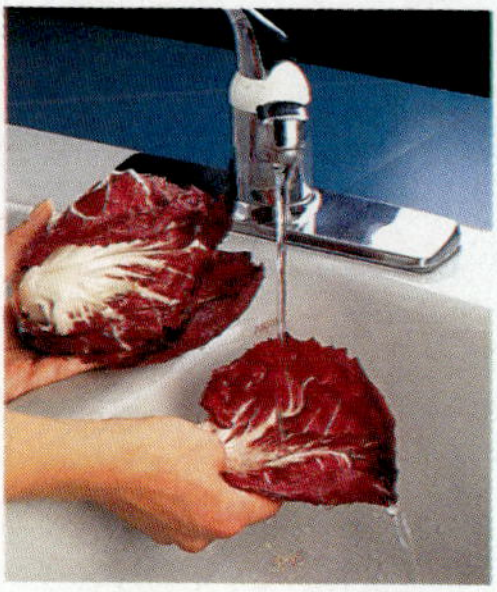

4. Arrange radicchio leaves, fennel and remaining olives on serving plate. Spoon dressing over salad. Garnish, if desired. Serve immediately.

Makes 4 servings

Marinated Vegetable Salad

- **3½ tablespoons white wine vinegar**
- **2 tablespoons minced fresh basil *or* ½ teaspoon dried basil leaves, crushed**
- **½ teaspoon salt**
- **⅛ teaspoon pepper**
- **Dash sugar**
- **6 tablespoons olive oil**
- **2 ripe medium tomatoes**
- **⅓ cup pitted green olives**
- **⅓ cup Italian- or Greek-style black olives**
- **1 head leaf or red leaf lettuce**
- **1 small head curly endive**
- **2 heads Belgian endive**

1. For dressing, place vinegar, basil, salt, pepper and sugar in food processor or blender. With motor running, add oil in slow steady stream until oil is thoroughly blended.

2. Cut tomatoes into quarters. Combine tomatoes and green and black olives in medium bowl. Add dressing; toss lightly. Cover and let stand at room temperature 30 minutes to blend flavors, stirring occasionally.

3. Rinse leaf lettuce and curly endive; drain well. Refrigerate greens until ready to assemble salad. Core Belgian endive and separate leaves; rinse and drain well.

4. To serve, layer leaf lettuce, curly endive and Belgian endive leaves in large, shallow serving bowl.

5. Remove tomatoes and olives with slotted spoon and place on top of greens. Spoon remaining dressing over salad. Serve immediately or cover and refrigerate up to 30 minutes.

Makes 6 servings

Fried Eggplant

1 medium eggplant (about 1 pound)
1 teaspoon salt
6 ounces mozzarella cheese
½ teaspoon active dry yeast
1½ cups warm water (105°F to 115°F)
2 cups all-purpose flour, divided
⅛ teaspoon pepper
4½ tablespoons olive oil, divided
2 tablespoons minced fresh basil *or* ½ teaspoon dried basil leaves, crushed
Vegetable oil
1 egg white
Lemon slices (optional)
Fresh basil leaf for garnish

1. Rinse eggplant; cut crosswise into ¼-inch-thick slices. Place in large colander over bowl; sprinkle with salt. Drain 1 hour.

2. Cut cheese into ⅛-inch-thick slices. Trim cheese slices to size of eggplant slices. Wrap in plastic; set aside.

3. Sprinkle yeast over warm water in medium bowl; stir until dissolved. Whisk in 1½ cups flour and pepper until smooth. Let batter stand at room temperature 30 minutes.

4. Rinse eggplant and drain well; pat slices dry between paper towels. Heat 1½ tablespoons olive oil in large skillet over medium-high heat; add as many eggplant slices in single layer without crowding to hot oil. Cook 2 minutes per side until slices are light brown. Remove with slotted spatula; drain on paper towels. Repeat with remaining olive oil and eggplant slices.

5. Sprinkle cheese slices with basil. Place each cheese slice between 2 eggplant slices; press firmly together. Spread remaining ½ cup flour on plate. Dip eggplant stacks in flour to coat lightly.

6. Heat 1½ inches vegetable oil in large saucepan to 350°F. Adjust heat to maintain temperature. Beat egg white in small bowl with electric mixer at high speed until stiff peaks form; fold into yeast batter. Dip eggplant stacks, 1 at a time, into batter; gently shake off excess. Fry stacks in oil, 3 at a time, 2 minutes per side until browned. Remove with slotted spatula; drain on paper towels.

Serve hot with lemon slices. Garnish, if desired.

Makes 4 to 6 servings

Spinach Gnocchi

- **2 packages (10 ounces) frozen chopped spinach**
- **1 cup ricotta cheese**
- **2 eggs**
- **⅔ cup freshly grated Parmesan cheese (about 2 ounces), divided**
- **1 cup *plus* 3 tablespoons all-purpose flour, divided**
- **½ teaspoon salt**
- **⅛ teaspoon pepper**
- **⅛ teaspoon ground nutmeg**
- **3 tablespoons butter or margarine, melted**

1. Cook spinach according to package directions. Drain well; let cool. Squeeze spinach dry; place in medium bowl. Stir in ricotta cheese. Add eggs; mix well. Add ⅓ cup Parmesan cheese, 3 tablespoons flour, salt, pepper and nutmeg; mix. Cover; refrigerate 1 hour.

2. Spread remaining 1 cup flour in shallow baking pan. Press a heaping tablespoonful of spinach mixture between a spoon and your hand to form oval gnocchi; place on flour. Repeat with remaining spinach mixture.

3. Roll gnocchi lightly in flour to coat evenly; discard excess flour. Drop 8 to 12 gnocchi into large pot of boiling salted water; reduce heat to medium.

4. Cook, uncovered, 5 minutes or until gnocchi are slightly puffed and slightly firm to the touch. Remove gnocchi with slotted spoon; drain on paper towels. Immediately transfer to greased *broilerproof* shallow baking dish. Reheat water to boiling. Repeat with remaining gnocchi in batches of 8 to 12. Arrange gnocchi in single layer in baking dish.

5. Preheat broiler. Spoon butter over gnocchi; sprinkle with remaining ⅓ cup Parmesan cheese. Broil gnocchi 5 inches from heat 2 to 3 minutes until cheese melts and browns lightly. Serve immediately. Garnish as desired.

Makes 4 to 6 servings (about 24 gnocchi)

Risotto alla Milanese

- **1/4 teaspoon saffron threads**
- **3 1/2 to 4 cups chicken broth**
- **7 tablespoons butter or margarine, divided**
- **1 large onion, chopped**
- **1 1/2 cups uncooked Arborio or short-grain white rice**
- **1/2 cup dry white wine**
- **1/2 teaspoon salt**
- **Dash pepper**
- **1/4 cup freshly grated Parmesan cheese**
- **Chopped fresh parsley, fresh parsley sprig and tomato slices for garnish**

1. Crush saffron in mortar with pestle to a powder.

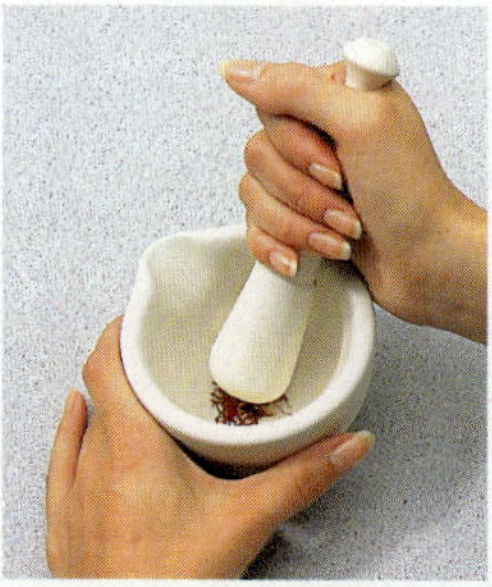

2. Bring broth to a boil in small saucepan over medium heat; reduce heat to low. Stir 1/2 cup broth into saffron to dissolve; set aside. Keep remaining broth hot.

3. Heat 6 tablespoons butter in large, heavy skillet or 2 1/2-quart saucepan over medium heat until melted and bubbly. Cook and stir onion in hot butter 5 minutes or until onion is soft. Stir in rice; cook and stir 2 minutes. Stir in wine, salt and pepper. Cook, uncovered, over medium-high heat 3 to 5 minutes until wine has evaporated, stirring occasionally.

4. Measure 1/2 cup hot broth; stir into rice mixture. Reduce heat to medium-low, maintaining a simmer throughout steps 4 and 5. Cook and stir until broth has absorbed. Repeat, adding 1/2 cup broth 3 more times, cooking and stirring until broth has absorbed.

5. Add saffron-flavored broth to rice and cook until absorbed. Continue adding remaining broth, 1/2 cup at a time, and cooking until rice is tender but firm and mixture has slightly creamy consistency. (Not all the broth may be necessary. Total cooking time of rice will be about 20 minutes.)

6. Remove risotto from heat. Stir in remaining 1 tablespoon butter and cheese. Garnish, if desired. Serve immediately.

Makes 6 to 8 servings

Classic Polenta

6 cups water
2 teaspoons salt
2 cups yellow cornmeal
¼ cup vegetable oil

1. Bring water and salt to a boil in large, heavy saucepan over medium-high heat. Stirring water vigorously, add cornmeal in very thin but steady stream (do not let lumps form). Reduce heat to low.

2. Cook polenta, uncovered, 40 to 60 minutes until very thick, stirring frequently. Polenta is ready when spoon will stand upright by itself in center of mixture. Polenta can be served at this point.*

3. For fried polenta, spray 11×7-inch baking pan with nonstick cooking spray. Spread polenta mixture evenly into baking pan. Cover and let stand at room temperature at least 6 hours or until completely cooled and firm.

4. Unmold polenta onto cutting board. Cut polenta crosswise into 1¼-inch-wide strips. Cut strips into 2- to 3-inch-long pieces.

5. Heat oil in large, heavy skillet over medium-high heat; reduce heat to medium. Fry polenta pieces, ½ at a time, 4 to 5 minutes until golden on all sides, turning as needed. Garnish as desired.

Makes 6 to 8 servings

*Polenta is an important component of Northern Italian cooking. The basic preparation presented here can be served in two forms. Hot freshly made polenta, prepared through step 2, can be mixed with ⅓ cup butter and ⅓ cup grated Parmesan cheese and served as a first course. Or, pour onto a large platter and top with Bolognese sauce (page 20) or other hearty meat sauces for a main dish. Fried polenta, as prepared here, is appropriate as an appetizer or as a side dish with meat.

Tiramisu

1 recipe Zabaglione (page 78)
⅔ cup heavy or whipping cream, chilled
4 tablespoons sugar, divided
1 pound mascarpone cheese* (about 2¼ cups)
⅓ cup freshly brewed espresso or strong coffee
¼ cup Cognac or brandy
1 tablespoon vanilla extract
3 packages (3 ounces each) ladyfingers, split
3 ounces bittersweet or semisweet chocolate, grated
1 tablespoon cocoa powder
Edible flowers, such as pansies, for garnish**

*Mascarpone is available at Italian markets and some specialty stores. If unavailable, blend 2 packages (8 ounces each) softened cream cheese with ½ cup heavy or whipping cream and 5 tablespoons sour cream.

** Be sure to use only non-toxic flowers.

1. Prepare Zabaglione. Cover and refrigerate until well chilled.

2. Beat cream with 2 tablespoons sugar in large bowl until soft peaks form. Gently fold in mascarpone cheese, then Zabaglione. (If Zabaglione has separated, beat until well mixed before folding into mascarpone.) Refrigerate 3 hours or until well chilled.

3. Combine espresso, cognac, remaining 2 tablespoons sugar and vanilla extract.

4. Layer ¼ of ladyfingers in flower-petal design in 2-quart glass bowl with straight sides or trifle dish.

5. Generously brush ladyfingers with espresso mixture. Spoon ¼ of cheese mixture over ladyfingers to within 1 inch of side of bowl. Sprinkle with ¼ of grated chocolate.

continued on page 78

Tiramisu, continued

6. Repeat layers 3 more times using remaining ladyfingers, espresso mixture and grated chocolate. (For garnish, sprinkle remaining 1/4 of grated chocolate around edge of dessert, if desired.) Sift cocoa powder over top with small sieve or tea strainer. Cover and

refrigerate at least 30 minutes or until chilled. Garnish, if desired.

Makes 8 to 10 servings

Zabaglione

5 egg yolks
1/4 cup sugar
1/2 cup marsala, divided
1/4 cup dry white wine

1. Place egg yolks in top of double boiler; add sugar. Beat with portable electric mixer at medium speed or rotary beater until mixture is pale yellow and creamy.

2. Place water in bottom of double boiler. Bring to a boil over high heat; reduce heat to low. Place top of double boiler over simmering water. Gradually beat 1/4 cup marsala into egg yolk mixture. Beat 1 minute. Gradually beat in remaining 1/4 cup marsala and white wine.

3. Continue cooking custard over gently simmering water 6 to 10 minutes until mixture is fluffy and thick enough to form soft mounds when dropped from beaters, beating constantly and scraping bottom and sides of pan frequently. (Watch carefully and *do not overcook* or custard will curdle.)

Immediately remove top of double boiler from water. Whisk custard briefly.***

*** Zabaglione can be served as its own recipe. Pour into 4 individual serving dishes. Serve immediately with fresh berries and/or cookies.

Makes 4 servings

Custard Rum Torte

6 eggs
1¼ cups granulated sugar, divided
¾ teaspoon salt, divided
1¼ cups all-purpose flour
⅓ cup cornstarch
3½ cups milk
2 egg yolks
2 tablespoons butter or margarine
2 teaspoons vanilla extract
2 pints fresh strawberries
6 tablespoons dark rum
4 cups heavy or whipping cream (2 pints)
¼ cup powdered sugar, sifted

1. For cake, preheat oven to 350°F. Grease and flour 10-inch springform pan. Beat eggs in large bowl with electric mixer at high speed until foamy. Beat in ¾ cup granulated sugar, 2 tablespoons at a time, beating well after each addition. Beat 3 minutes more. Beat in ¼ teaspoon salt. Sift ⅓ of flour over egg mixture; fold in. Repeat until all flour has been incorporated.

2. Spread batter evenly into prepared springform pan. Bake 40 minutes or until wooden toothpick inserted in center comes out clean. Cool in pan on wire rack 10 minutes. Loosen cake from side of pan with tip of knife; remove side of pan. Remove cake from bottom of pan to wire rack. Cool completely. Clean pan.

3. For custard, combine remaining ½ cup granulated sugar, cornstarch and remaining ½ teaspoon salt in large saucepan; mix well. Stir in milk until smooth. Bring to a boil over medium heat, stirring frequently. Boil 3 minutes, stirring constantly; remove from heat. Whisk egg yolks in small bowl; gradually whisk in 1 cup hot milk mixture. Gradually whisk egg yolk mixture into remaining milk mixture in saucepan. Cook over low heat 1 minute, stirring constantly. Immediately pour custard into medium bowl. Cut butter into 6 pieces; add to custard and stir until melted. Stir in vanilla extract. Press waxed paper onto surface of custard; refrigerate. Cool completely.

continued on page 80

Custard Rum Torte, continued

4. Rinse and drain strawberries. Reserve 8 whole strawberries; wrap in plastic wrap and refrigerate for garnish. Hull and thinly slice remaining strawberries.

5. To cut cooled cake horizontally into 3 even layers, measure with ruler into 3 equal layers and mark with wooden toothpicks. Cut through cake with thin serrated knife using toothpicks as guide.

6. To assemble, brush top of each layer with 2 tablespoons rum. Place one cake layer in bottom of cleaned springform pan. Spread evenly with ½ of custard. Arrange ½ of strawberry slices over custard in single layer. Top with second cake layer; spread with remaining custard and top with remaining strawberry slices. Place third cake layer on top. Cover and refrigerate at least 12 hours.

7. About 45 minutes before serving, beat cream with powdered sugar in large bowl with electric mixer at high speed until stiff. Spoon 2 cups whipped cream mixture into pastry bag fitted with large star tip; refrigerate. Remove side of pan; place dessert on serving plate (do not remove bottom of pan). Spread remaining whipped cream mixture evenly and smoothly on sides and top of dessert. Pipe reserved whipped cream mixture around top and bottom edges of dessert. Refrigerate 30 minutes before serving.

8. To serve, garnish with reserved whole strawberries. Cut dessert into slices. Refrigerate leftovers.

Makes 10 to 12 servings

Fig and Hazelnut Cake

¾ cup hazelnuts or filberts (about 4 ounces)
3 ounces semisweet chocolate
⅔ cup slivered blanched almonds (about 3 ounces), coarsely chopped
¾ cup whole dried figs (about 4 ounces), coarsely chopped
⅓ cup diced candied orange peel
⅓ cup diced candied lemon peel
3 eggs
½ cup sugar
1¼ cups all-purpose flour
1¾ teaspoons baking powder
¾ teaspoon salt

1. Preheat oven to 350°F. To remove skins from hazelnuts, spread hazelnuts in single layer on baking sheet. Bake 10 to 12 minutes until toasted and skins begin to flake off; let cool slightly. Wrap hazelnuts in heavy kitchen towel; rub against towel to remove as much of the skins as possible.

2. Coarsely chop hazelnuts. Finely chop chocolate. Combine hazelnuts, almonds, figs, candied orange and lemon peels and chocolate in medium bowl; mix well.

3. *Reduce oven temperature to 300°F.* Grease 8×4-inch loaf pan.

4. Beat eggs and sugar in large bowl with electric mixer at high speed at least 5 minutes or until mixture is pale yellow and thick and fluffy. Gently fold nut mixture into egg mixture.

5. Combine flour, baking powder and salt in small bowl. Sift ½ of flour mixture over nut-egg mixture and gently fold in; repeat with remaining flour mixture.

6. Spread batter evenly into prepared pan. Bake 60 to 70 minutes until top is deep golden brown and firm to the touch. Cool in pan on wire rack 5 minutes. Remove loaf from pan; cool completely on wire rack at least 4 hours. Slice and serve.

Makes 12 to 16 servings

Cannoli Pastries

18 to 20 Cannoli Pastry Shells (recipe follows)
2 pounds ricotta cheese
1½ cups sifted powdered sugar
2 teaspoons ground cinnamon
¼ cup diced candied orange peel, minced
1 teaspoon grated lemon peel
Powdered sugar
2 ounces semisweet chocolate, finely chopped
Orange peel strips and fresh mint leaves for garnish

1. Prepare Cannoli Pastry Shells; set aside.

2. For cannoli filling, beat cheese in large bowl with electric mixer at medium speed until smooth. Add 1½ cups powdered sugar and cinnamon; beat at high speed 3 minutes. Add candied orange peel and lemon peel to cheese mixture; mix well. Cover and refrigerate until ready to serve.

3. To assemble, spoon cheese filling into pastry bag fitted with large plain tip. Pipe about ¼ cup filling into each reserved cannoli pastry shell.*

4. Roll Cannoli Pastries in additional powdered sugar to coat. Dip ends of pastries into chocolate. Arrange pastries on serving plate. Garnish, if desired.

Makes 18 to 20 pastries

*Do not fill Cannoli Pastry Shells ahead of time or shells will become soggy.

Cannoli Pastry Shells

1¾ cups all-purpose flour
2 tablespoons granulated sugar
1 teaspoon grated lemon peel
2 tablespoons butter or margarine, cold
1 egg
6 tablespoons marsala
Vegetable oil

1. Mix flour, granulated sugar and lemon peel in medium bowl; cut in butter with 2 knives or pastry blender until mixture resembles fine crumbs. Beat egg and marsala in small bowl; add to flour mixture. Stir with fork to form ball. Divide dough in half; shape into two 1-inch-thick square pieces. Wrap in plastic wrap and refrigerate at least 1 hour.

continued on page 86

Cannoli Pastries, continued

2. Heat 1½ inches oil in large saucepan to 325°F. Working with 1 piece of dough at a time, roll out on lightly floured surface to 1/16-inch thickness. Cut dough with knife into 9 or 10 (4 × 3-inch) rectangles.

3. Wrap each rectangle around a greased metal cannoli form or uncooked cannelloni pasta shell. Brush one edge of rectangle lightly with water; overlap with other edge and press firmly to seal.

4. Fry, 2 or 3 cannoli pastry shells at a time, 1 to 1½ minutes until light brown, turning once. Remove with tongs; drain on paper towels.

5. Cool until easy to handle. Carefully remove fried pastries from cannoli forms or pasta shells; cool completely. Repeat with remaining piece of dough.

Florentine Cookies

- **¼ cup sliced blanched almonds**
- **¼ cup walnuts**
- **5 red candied cherries**
- **1 tablespoon golden or dark raisins**
- **1 tablespoon diced candied lemon peel**
- **1 tablespoon crystallized ginger**
- **¼ cup unsalted butter**
- **¼ cup sugar**
- **1 tablespoon heavy or whipping cream**
- **3 tablespoons all-purpose flour**
- **4 ounces semisweet chocolate**

1. Finely chop almonds, walnuts, cherries, raisins, lemon peel and ginger; combine in small bowl. Set aside.

2. Preheat oven to 350°F. Grease 2 large baking sheets.

3. Combine butter, sugar and cream in small, heavy saucepan. Cook, uncovered, over medium heat until sugar dissolves and mixture boils, stirring constantly. Cook and stir 1 minute more. Remove from heat. Stir in reserved nut-fruit mixture. Add flour; mix well.

4. Spoon heaping teaspoon batter onto prepared baking sheet. Repeat, placing 4 cookies on each baking sheet to allow room for spreading.

continued on page 88

Florentine Cookies, continued

5. Bake cookies, 1 baking sheet at a time, 8 to 10 minutes until deep brown. Remove baking sheet from oven to wire rack. If cookies have spread unevenly, push in edges with metal spatula to round out shape. Cool cookies 1 minute or until firm enough to remove from sheet, then quickly but carefully remove cookies with wide metal spatula to wire racks. Cool completely.

6. Repeat with remaining batter. (To prevent cookies from spreading too quickly, allow baking sheets to cool before greasing and spooning batter onto sheets.)

7. Finely chop chocolate. Bring water in bottom of double boiler just to a boil; remove from heat. Place chocolate in top of double boiler and place over water. Stir chocolate until melted; immediately remove from water. Let chocolate cool slightly.

8. Line large baking sheet with waxed paper. Turn cookies over; spread chocolate on bottoms. Place cookies, chocolate side up, on prepared baking sheet; let stand until chocolate is almost set. Score chocolate in zig-zag pattern with tines of fork.

Let stand until completely set or refrigerate until firm. Serve or store in airtight container in refrigerator. Garnish as desired.

Makes about 2 dozen cookies

Classic Anise Biscotti

4 ounces whole blanched almonds (about 3/4 cup)
2 1/4 cups all-purpose flour
1 teaspoon baking powder
3/4 teaspoon salt
3/4 cup sugar
1/2 cup unsalted butter, softened
3 eggs
2 tablespoons brandy
2 teaspoons grated lemon peel
1 tablespoon whole anise seeds

1. Preheat oven to 375°F. To toast almonds, spread almonds on baking sheet. Bake 6 to 8 minutes until toasted and light brown; turn off oven. Remove almonds with spoon to cutting board; cool. Coarsely chop almonds.

2. Combine flour, baking powder and salt in small bowl. Beat sugar and butter in medium bowl with electric mixer at medium speed until light and fluffy. Add eggs, 1 at a time, beating well after each addition and scraping sides of bowl often. Stir in brandy and lemon peel. Add flour mixture gradually; stir until smooth. Stir in almonds and anise seeds. Cover and refrigerate dough 1 hour or until firm.

3. Preheat oven to 375°F. Grease large baking sheet. Divide dough in half. Shape 1/2 of dough into 12×2-inch log on lightly floured surface. (Dough will be fairly soft.) Pat smooth with lightly floured fingertips. Repeat with remaining 1/2 of dough to form second log. Bake 20 to 25 minutes until logs are light golden brown. Remove baking sheet from oven to wire rack; turn off oven. Cool logs completely.

4. Preheat oven to 350°F. Cut logs diagonally with serrated knife into 1/2-inch-thick slices. Place slices flat in single layer on 2 ungreased baking sheets.

5. Bake 8 minutes. Turn slices over; bake 10 to 12 minutes more until cut surfaces are light brown and cookies are dry. Remove cookies to wire racks; cool completely. Store cookies in airtight container up to 2 weeks.

Makes about 4 dozen cookies

Italian Ice

1 cup sweet or dry fruity white wine
1 cup water
1 cup sugar
1 cup lemon juice
2 egg whites
Fresh berries (optional)
Mint leaves for garnish

1. Place wine and water in small saucepan; add sugar. Cook over medium-high heat until sugar has dissolved and syrup boils, stirring frequently. Cover; boil 1 minute. Uncover; adjust heat to maintain simmer. Simmer 10 minutes without stirring. Remove from heat. Refrigerate 1 hour or until syrup is completely cool.

2. Stir lemon juice into cooled syrup. Pour into 9-inch round cake pan. Freeze 1 hour.

3. Quickly stir mixture with fork breaking up ice crystals. Freeze 1 hour more or until firm but not solid. Meanwhile, place medium bowl in freezer to chill.

4. Beat egg whites in small bowl with electric mixer at high speed until stiff peaks form. Remove lemon ice mixture from cake pan to chilled bowl. Immediately beat ice with whisk or fork until smooth. Fold in egg whites; mix well. Spread egg mixture evenly into same cake pan. Freeze 30 minutes. Immediately stir with fork; cover cake pan with foil. Freeze at least 3 hours or until firm.

5. To serve, scoop Italian Ice into fluted champagne glasses or dessert dishes. Serve with berries. Garnish, if desired.

Makes 4 servings

INDEX

Antipasto with Marinated
  Mushrooms, 10

Appetizers (*see also* **Soups**)
- Antipasto with Marinated Mushrooms, 10
- Fried Calamari with Tartar Sauce, 56
- Marinated Mushrooms, 10
- Mediterranean Frittata, 8
- Venetian Canapés, 6

Beans
- Minestrone alla Milanese, 18

Beef
- Classic Meatball Soup, 16
- Four-Meat Ravioli, 24
- Spaghetti alla Bolognese, 20
- Spinach Lasagna, 33

Canapés, Venetian, 6
Cannoli Pastries, 84
Cannoli Pastry Shells, 84

Cheese
- Antipasto with Marinated Mushrooms, 10
- Cannoli Pastries, 84
- Classic Chicken Marsala, 52
- Classic Fettuccine Alfredo, 36
- Classic Veal Florentine, 44
- Fettuccine alla Carbonara, 22
- Fried Eggplant, 68
- Homemade Pizza, 59
- Spinach Gnocchi, 70
- Spinach Lasagna, 33
- Tiramisu, 76
- Tomato, Mozzarella & Basil Salad, 62
- Veal Parmesan, 48

Chicken
- Chicken Cacciatore, 50
- Chicken Tortellini with Mushroom-Cream Sauce, 27
- Classic Chicken Marsala, 52
- Four-Meat Ravioli, 24

Chocolate
- Fig and Hazelnut Cake, 82
- Florentine Cookies, 87
- Tiramisu, 76

Cioppino, 13
Classic Anise Biscotti, 90
Classic Chicken Marsala, 52
Classic Fettuccine Alfredo, 36
Classic Meatball Soup, 16
Classic Pesto with Linguine, 42
Classic Polenta, 74
Classic Veal Florentine, 44

Cookies
- Classic Anise Biscotti, 90
- Florentine Cookies, 87

Custard Rum Torte, 79

Desserts (*see also* **Cookies**)
- Cannoli Pastries, 84
- Custard Rum Torte, 79
- Fig and Hazelnut Cake, 82
- Italian Ice, 92
- Tiramisu, 76
- Zabaglione, 78

Eggplant, Fried, 68

Fennel, Olive and Radicchio Salad, 64
Fettuccine alla Carbonara, 22
Fig and Hazelnut Cake, 82
Fish (*see* **Seafood**)
Fish alla Milanese, 54
Florentine Cookies, 87
Four-Meat Ravioli, 24
Fried Calamari with Tartar Sauce, 56
Fried Eggplant, 68

Homemade Angel Hair Pasta with Classic Tomato Sauces, 39
Homemade Fettuccine, 36
Homemade Pizza, 59

Italian Ice, 92

Lasagna, Spinach, 33

Marinated Mushrooms, 10
Marinated Vegetable Salad, 66
Mediterranean Frittata, 8
Minestrone alla Milanese, 18

Mushrooms
Antipasto with Marinated Mushrooms, 10
Chicken Cacciatore, 50
Chicken Tortellini with Mushroom-Cream Sauce, 27
Marinated Mushrooms, 10
Spinach Lasagna, 33
Veal Scallopine, 46
Venetian Canapés, 6

Neapolitan Sauce, 40
Nuts
Classic Anise Biscotti, 90
Fig and Hazelnut Cake, 82
Florentine Cookies, 87

Pancetta
Fettuccine alla Carbonara, 22
Pasta
Chicken Tortellini with Mushroom-Cream Sauce, 27
Classic Fettuccine Alfredo, 36
Classic Meatball Soup, 16
Classic Pesto with Linguine, 42
Fettuccine alla Carbonara, 22
Four-Meat Ravioli, 24
Homemade Angel Hair Pasta with Classic Tomato Sauces, 39
Homemade Fettuccine, 36
Spaghetti alla Bolognese, 20
Spaghetti with Seafood Marinara Sauce, 30
Spinach Lasagna, 33
Pizza, Homemade, 59
Pizzaiola Sauce, 40
Plum Tomato Sauce, 26
Polenta, Classic, 74
Pork (*see* **Pancetta; Prosciutto**)
Prosciutto
Antipasto with Marinated Mushrooms, 10
Chicken Tortellini with Mushroom-Cream Sauce, 27
Four-Meat Ravioli, 24
Mediterranean Frittata, 8

Risotto alla Milanese, 72

Salads
Fennel, Olive and Radicchio Salad, 64
Marinated Vegetable Salad, 66
Tomato, Mozzarella & Basil Salad, 62
Sauces
Classic Pesto with Linguine, 42
Neapolitan Sauce, 40
Pizzaiola Sauce, 40
Plum Tomato Sauce, 26
Tartar Sauce, 58
Seafood
Cioppino, 13
Fish alla Milanese, 54
Fried Calamari with Tartar Sauce, 56
Spaghetti with Seafood Marinara Sauce, 30
Shellfish (*see* **Seafood**)
Side Dishes (*see also* **Salads**)
Classic Polenta, 74
Fried Eggplant, 68
Risotto alla Milanese, 72
Spinach Gnocchi, 70
Soups
Cioppino, 13
Classic Meatball Soup, 16
Minestrone alla Milanese, 18
Spaghetti alla Bolognese, 20
Spaghetti with Seafood Marinara Sauce, 30
Spinach
Chicken Tortellini with Mushroom-Cream Sauce, 27
Classic Veal Florentine, 44
Four-Meat Ravioli, 24
Spinach Gnocchi, 70
Spinach Lasagna, 33

Tartar Sauce, 58
Tiramisu, 76
Tomato, Mozzarella & Basil Salad, 62

Veal
Classic Veal Florentine, 44
Veal Parmesan, 48
Veal Scallopine, 46
Vegetables (*see* **Beans; Eggplant; Mushrooms; Salads; Spinach**)
Venetian Canapés, 6

Zabaglione, 78

METRIC CONVERSION CHART

VOLUME MEASUREMENT (dry)

⅛ teaspoon = .5 mL
¼ teaspoon = 1 mL
½ teaspoon = 2 mL
¾ teaspoon = 4 mL
1 teaspoon = 5 mL
1 tablespoon = 15 mL
2 tablespoons = 25 mL
¼ cup = 50 mL
⅓ cup = 75 mL
⅔ cup = 150 mL
¾ cup = 175 mL
1 cup = 250 mL
2 cups = 1 pint = 500 mL
3 cups = 750 mL
4 cups = 1 quart = 1 L

VOLUME MEASUREMENT (fluid)

1 fluid ounce (2 tablespoons) = 30 mL
4 fluid ounces (½ cup) = 125 mL
8 fluid ounces (1 cup) = 250 mL
12 fluid ounces (1½ cups) = 375 mL
16 fluid ounces (2 cups) = 500 mL

WEIGHT (MASS)

½ ounce = 15 g
1 ounce = 30 g
3 ounces = 85 g
3.75 ounces = 100 g
4 ounces = 115 g
8 ounces = 225 g
12 ounces = 340 g
16 ounces = 1 pound = 450 g

DIMENSION

1/16 inch = 2 mm
⅛ inch = 3 mm
¼ inch = 6 mm
½ inch = 1.5 cm
¾ inch = 2 cm
1 inch = 2.5 cm

OVEN TEMPERATURES

250°F = 120°C
275°F = 140°C
300°F = 150°C
325°F = 160°C
350°F = 180°C
375°F = 190°C
400°F = 200°C
425°F = 220°C
450°F = 230°C

BAKING PAN SIZES

Utensil	Inches/ Quarts	Metric Volume	Centimeters
Baking or	8×8×2	2 L	20×20×5
Cake pan	9×9×2	2.5 L	22×22×5
(square or	12×8×2	3 L	30×20×5
rectangular)	13×9×2	3.5 L	33×23×5
Loaf Pan	8×4×3	1.5 L	20×10×7
	9×5×3	2 L	23×13×7
Round Layer	8×1½	1.2 L	20×4
Cake Pan	9×1½	1.5 L	23×4
Pie Plate	8×1¼	750 mL	20×3
	9×1¼	1 L	23×3
Baking Dish	1 quart	1 L	
or	1½ quart	1.5 L	
Casserole	2 quart	2 L	